Domestic Olympics

The Ultimate Housecleaning Guide

Richard A. Slinde

iUniverse, Inc.
Bloomington

Domestic Olympics
The Ultimate Housecleaning Guide

iUniverse books may be ordered through booksellers or by contacting:

iUniverse
1663 Liberty Drive
Bloomington, IN 47403
www.iuniverse.com
1-800-Authors (1-800-288-4677)

ISBN: 978-1-4697-7745-0 (sc)
ISBN: 978-1-4697-7746-7 (hc)
ISBN: 978-1-4697-7747-4 (e)

Library of Congress Control Number: 2012902573

Printed in the United States of America

iUniverse rev. date: 2/8/2012

Contents

Acknowledgments

For Christel and Carol

Introduction

I wanted to write this book because there didn't seem to be any books taking you on a step by step journey through the home. After checking in my local library for what was out there and looking onto the open market, for what was available, I came to the conclusion that there was a spot in the market for what I had to offer. My friends had been asking me for years to write down how to clean this or that. So I decided that it was time for me to finally take action. The answers to all of their questions are answered within.

As a young boy, my chores around the house consisted of washing windows, mowing the lawn, and cleaning the basement. Occasionally something else might be thrown in to keep me busy—like taking out the trash.

Of course, my allowance encouraged me to finish up those chores in a hurry. But as a young boy, I wanted to be outside running around with my friends.

We all hate the chores around the house but know that they need to be done, even though they're a pain in the butt. By keeping our homes and our lives on schedule, we free ourselves up for those moments that are important to us.

These chores prepared me for a career later in life as a maintenance engineer for a large apartment complex outside of Chicago. Fifteen buildings were my world! My life involved everything from cleaning the halls to repairing frozen pipes in the winter, along with cleaning vacant units. I met a very important person at this time. She and I became the best of friends, and we did everything together. When the owner of the complex decided to go condo in the late seventies, we chose to go into business together. In December 1979, we started our company, C and R Cleaning Inc. Our first contract was the conversion of 125 buildings.

We cleaned the vacant units, hallways, model apartments, offices, and newly restored units before move-ins were final. For over thirty years now the business has included many departments, from single units to high-rises. Then there is the commercial end of the business—working for banks and developers, new construction cleaning, and much more. After my partner passed in 1996, I closed down the commercial end of the business and kept the residential end working.

Life experiences have pushed me in the direction of writing down what I know will be of help to others. This is a very honest, straightforward approach to cleaning your home, with tips along the way to make your life a little easier; it's a step-by-step guide to cleaning just about everything you can think of and then some.

Getting started—
What's in Your Bucket

Cleaning your home is not rocket science, but at times it does take science to solve your cleaning dilemmas. Finding the perfect methods for cleaning your house seems like a daunting prospect, but most problems can be solved with a little know-how. *Domestic Olympics: The Ultimate Housecleaning Guide* puts forth a simple plan that anyone can use by adjusting it to their circumstances. Whether your accommodations are modest or grand, this book will make your life a little easier and your home a more comfortable place. There will be plenty of repetition within this book. The reason for it is to get you to remember the steps that must be taken. Cleaning is very repetitious, but once you have it down, it will stay with you forever. So don't be afraid of the repetition.

So let's get started. Here is a list of what is in my bucket. Put them into yours, and you'll be set to go.

1. A two-gallon bucket
2. A brass squeegee for windows and mirrors
3. A good scrub brush
4. A bottle of tilex mold and mildew remover for the bath
5. A bottle of your favorite window cleaner
6. A bottle of Lysol bacterial disinfectant (yellow color)
7. A bottle of Mrs. Meyer's all-purpose cleaner
8. A plastic cup for rinsing down shower walls
9. A small container filled with laundry detergent (powder form only)
10. A large sponge with a scratch pad on one side
11. Microfiber cloths for washing and dusting
12. A good vacuum with attachments
13. A mop that rings out well
14. A cob-web duster
15. A razor-blade scraper

These are the items in my bucket. After thirty years, of being in the cleaning business believe me, I've got it down to a precise science. It seems like a lot of things, but they will last a long time; all you will have to do is replace them when necessary.

Of course, there are many other cleaning products to choose from: products for silver, copper, crystal, acrylic, and so forth. We will list them in another chapter and explain what to expect from each of them.

For the purpose of this book, I'm setting up a home with one bathroom, three bedrooms, a living room, a dining room, a kitchen and a family room, along with an entryway and laundry room. If you can follow the plan outlined in this book, you can clean anything. Believe me; I've worked on spaces as small as one room up to and including thirty-room homes.

This is the beginning. Let there be light. Turn on the lights because you can't see the dirt in the dark.

Cleaning Products—
Choosing the Right Target

Finding the right cleaning product can be overwhelming. There are so many cleaners on the market; who knows which one is the right one? We are going to travel through this galaxy of products and hope we don't get thrown into a wormhole and go even farther into the darkness. Let's start by talking about the products I recommended in "The Beginning"; the products that are in my bucket and the ones in my car that get used occasionally. I am a firm believer in keeping it simple. The basics that I have put into my bucket are just that—basic. You can expand on or omit these products as needed.

Powdered Detergent
It really doesn't matter which brand you choose. Powdered detergent is filled with enzymes, those little buggers that munch on all kinds of dirt and

grease. What a magical product! Who would have thought that this simple product would have so many uses, especially in the kitchen where it is used for grease removal, and in the bathroom where we use it for removal of soap and oil deposits? it is one of my favorite cleaning products.

Tilex Mold and Mildew Remover

This is a chemical-based product that everyone needs. It is not fun to have around, especially if you have children, so keep this one out of their reach. The product does exactly what it says: it takes care of mold and mildew. After you clean your bath, spray this wherever you see little black dots (i.e., the signs of mold and mildew), and let it stand until it is dry; do not rinse it off. It needs to stay on to do its job, which of course is removing the mold and mildew and turning your grout and caulking back to the white you like to see. Wear gloves when working with chemicals. And make sure the bathroom is ventilated. Also keep the spray away from chrome as it will damage those pieces. Just be careful, and it will work.

Window Cleaner

Once again, there are many brands to choose from, so simply pick your favorite as they all work the same. Alternatively, you may want to make your own. To do that, start with a new plastic bottle with a sprayer on it, the smaller the better. Run the hot water, fill the bottle, add five to six drops of liquid detergent, and tighten the sprayer, and you're ready to clean your windows. This is what a professional window washer I know uses. We use the liquid detergent because it cuts through the grease that has attached itself to the windows.

Lysol Cleaner

This is a bacterial disinfectant every house needs to help keep the germs away. Lysol is relatively inexpensive, and I have found it to be one of the best on the market. This is what you should use to clean your doorknobs, kitchen pulls and handles, telephones, keyboards, and remote controls as well as most of your home.

By the way, you likely can't all keep your hands in water all day as I do, but try to wash your hands as often as possible. Hand washing keeps away some pretty nasty germs.

Mrs. Meyers

What a great product for the shower! It's totally natural and fresh smelling and has lots of lemon oil. Spraying the walls and floor with Mrs. Meyers and then going over them with a scrubbing sponge and some liquid detergent will remove soap scum. Spray the walls and doors after you finish showering to keep the dirt in check.

This product is good for all hard surfaces, just remember to rinse and dry to stop streaking.

Don't forget a cup for rinsing the walls in the bathtub and shower. I use a plastic drinking cup, which holds enough water to do the job well.

Squeegee

There are many versions of this product; stick to the one that works best. Brass squeegees last forever, and you can change out the rubber when it needs to be replaced. If you have lots of windows of varying sizes, then you may want to purchase several sizes, from small to large. Believe me when I say you can be done in fast order with one of these, and your windows or mirrors will sparkle.

Scrubbing Brushes

There are many sizes and shapes of scrubbing brushes. They can do a lot of jobs, from scrubbing fingernails to sweeping out the garage and everything in between. I use a brush intended for scrubbing dishes to clean around the house. It works for most jobs in the house and can be replaced very inexpensively. Don't be afraid to use brushes; they can get into and clean the smallest places. Any time you have a job that seems hard to get at, think about using a brush. If you need to get under the fridge, there's a brush for that. If you need to get behind the washer, dryer, and baseboards, there's also a brush for those . There's a brush for the walls too. Think of any use, and there will be a brush waiting to be found. Don't be afraid to experiment; a brush can save you a lot of time.

Mop and Bucket
Any good hand-wringing mop and basic bucket will do. Keep them simple and inexpensive.

Vacuum Cleaner
Of course, you already know what I'm going to say: keep it simple and don't go crazy. Because I vacuum a lot, I need something that is a workhorse, while you will vacuum only when needed. Find a vacuum cleaner that is in the average to expensive price range. Make sure it has attachments and doesn't weigh as much as a truck. If you can't pick it up, it won't do you much good. My Oreck weighs about eight pounds and is used in most hotels.

The List
Well, those are the basics and what they do. Now let's turn our attention to products that you will use less often, which are listed below, alphabetically by subject matter. If you are looking for a good cleaner for silver, look under "S," and if you need

something to clean acrylic, look under "A." There are hundreds and possibly thousands of cleaners in the marketplace; I have listed what I know works. You can also experiment with other products to find the ones that will work best for you. I've tried hundreds of products over the past thirty years, and I'm still learning. There is always something new. And, of course, you'll be able to make some products yourself.

A

Acrylic: number one a brand name is for cleaning; number two removes fine scratches; number three removes heavy scratches. After using number three, finish by using number two.

Brilliance is a one-stop cleaner for plastics, aircraft, boats, mirrors, showcases, sneeze guards, television screens, chandelier crystals, fiberglass, refrigerators, glazed ceramic, polished granite, and medical and dental equipment.

Ants: The most important bit of information to remember when it comes to ants is this: keep the area clean. Wherever you find the ants, wash down the area with soap and water to remove the trace they leave behind as they move about. You can always use ant traps, or you can just wipe down your kitchen and pantry with a mixture of vinegar and water. The ants will then be repelled. If your infestation is out of control, you may want a professional to come in and spray for you and bait the area. Another good idea is to put bay leaves in the areas where you find ants, like drawers. Ants do not like the smell of the leaves.

B

Blinds: There many types of blinds, including mini, vertical, and Venetian, and there are three ways of cleaning them.

1. Get your gloves out and fill a bucket with warm water, a squirt of liquid soap, and a dash of bleach. Add your microfiber cloth, wring it out, and starting at the top corner, wipe each slat on both sides at once. Work your way to the bottom of the blind, then go to the next section, and move from the top down. Rinse your cloth out by rinsing it in the bucket several times, if need be. Continue until you have worked your way across the entire blind.

2. Verticals are done the same way, from top to bottom and side to side. Wipe the entire length of the vertical on both sides at once. If your verticles are fabric then you will

want to clean them with a fabric cleaner to remove spots. Then go over them with a steamer.

3. If you want to send your blinds out to be cleaned, ultrasonic cleaning is the method that works the best. This process will remove all dirt from the blinds and they will be returned to you like new. This website for a firm near Chicago, www.lovittblinds.com, contains information on this subject. Then look for a company in your area that does this type of work.

Blood: Bloodstains are the worst to get out, but they can come out. Equal parts of water and ammonia will do it. Just put the ammonia/water mixture on a sponge, wring it out over the blood, and let it sit for a moment, and then take a dry towel and blot it up. You may need to do this more than once to remove all of the blood. If you have blood on your clothes, take a wet sponge, add some hydrogen peroxide, and then wring the sponge out over the spot; then blot it out with a dry towel. A good wash afterward should complete the job.

Brass: Two good products for cleaning brass are Brasso and Wenol.

1. Brasso is a very good product. Just pour some onto a rag, and start wiping your brass;

scrubbing a little harder on discolored spots will remove them. Let the product dry; then wipe off with a clean, dry rag (T-shirts do a great job). See www.amazon.com to purchase.

2. Wenol is a high-end cleaner. I found it in a brass store in Chicago years ago. I watched as the store owner went from piece to piece cleaning the brass. It comes in a paste; rub it on, let it dry, and wipe it off. The brass will shine like glass when you are done. This metal polish can be purchased online (see www. autogeek.net).

Brick: tri-sodium phosphate is a great cleaner for brick. Wear gloves when using this product. Mix as directed, scrub the brick, and then rinse with clear water.

Copperfield (www.copperfield.com) is a company in Iowa that supply to the trades. Its masonry cleaner is the best. If you hire a professional to clean your brick, make sure the company uses this product.

Bronze: The only thing you need to clean bronze pieces, including outside statuary, is plain old Ivory liquid soap, water, and perhaps a toothbrush to get into crevices. Fill a bucket with warm water, add some Ivory, and wash the piece down. Rinse off all the soap, and let it dry for a couple of hours. Then use some tree wax or clear Johnson's paste wax, and apply it to your piece to protect it. Buff, if you must. Between cleanings, use a damp rag that has been wrung out so dry, if you shook it, dust would fly.

C

Carpets: To clean a spot or a spill on a carpet, take a towel, put it over the spot or spill, and step on it to absorb the liquid. Then dip a brush into a soap-and-water mixture, and rub lightly onto the spot or spill. Take another towel, and dry out the liquid to see if the spot or spill has been removed. If not, move onto the next step. Mix some powdered laundry detergent in warm water. Repeat the actions listed above.

If this does not work, use the heavy artillery. I like to use Woolite carpet cleaner spray. It's worked for me for years. Just spray, and work it into the spot or spill. Let it stand until you are ready to vacuum; then go over it with the vacuum cleaner, which should pull up the nap, and the spot or spill should be gone.

Another good carpet cleaner is a Bio Green Clean, available from www.biogreenclean.com. I recently started using it, and it's great. I used it on some spots the other day, and they came right out. Just spray, use a brush, and blot with a towel. The spot or spill should be gone; all those little enzymes will work their magic for you.

Cement: Many countertops are made from cement. Cleaning them is an easy process. Just use warm water and soap. Rinse them down with warm water and dry. If you need to reseal and polish follow your installer's directions. This usually means removing all stains, applying the sealer, and then polishing once everything has dried.

Ceramic tile: If the tile is on a floor, vacuum it first, or sweep it clean. Dissolve a quarter cup of powdered detergent in a bucket of warm water. Wet a microfiber cloth, wring it out, and wipe down the floor. Work your way out of the room you are cleaning.

Another method is to fill a bucket with warm water and add a cup of vinegar. Then, using the process above, wipe down the tiles. If they are on a wall, start at the top and work your way down.

Copper: I've used Twinkle (available from www. amazon.com) for years because it's simple and easy to use. Wipe it on, rinse it off, and dry; what could be easier? To make your own home remedy, use even amounts of salt, white vinegar, and flour. Just mix it into a paste and rub it over the copper. If the amounts are too small then add more until you have enough to finish the piece. Let it stand for ten minutes to an hour; then rinse and dry thoroughly.

Corian: Use warm, soapy water to clean; then rinse and dry. Do not use window cleaners on these surfaces. To disinfect, use one part water and one part bleach; then rinse and dry.

Crystal: Fill a large plastic bowl with warm water and some liquid soap. Wet a microfiber cloth with this mixture. To prevent breakage, put a towel in the bottom of the sink and another on the countertop, just in case you drop a piece. Take a piece of crystal, and rinse it off. Use the microfiber cloth to wash each piece; then rinse it clean of any soap, and place it on the towel to dry. Once you've covered the towel on the countertop, use a lint-free towel to dry the pieces. Return them to their rightful places. I've learned over the years that crystal gets brittle and needs to be placed in water to stop that process. That may be just an old wives' tale, but a couple of times a year, in and out of the sink is a good thing.

D

Dishwasher: Most people forget that the inside of their dishwasher needs to be attended to once in a while. A filtering system at the bottom of the unit is there to catch the excess food that drops away while the dishes are being cleaned. (That's the reason for rinsing out dishes before putting them into the unit.)

Take a microfiber cloth, run it over the filter, and pull out any particles that may be stuck there.

If your area has hard water, and rust has developed in the unit, then pour in a half a bottle of Lime-A-Way (www.limeaway.com) and run the unit twice. After the second wash, all rust should have been removed; if not, repeat the process. When that is done, put in a cup of bleach, and run it several times again. That should solve the problem.

Disposal: You might think that this unit does not need to be cleaned, but you'd be wrong. The buildup of odors from your disposal can radiate into your home and make life very unpleasant. Here's a method I've used for a very long time. Place your sink stopper in the sink; then fill the sink with water, almost to the top. Add about a quarter of a cup dishwashing liquid and the same amount of baking soda. Pull out the plug; turn on the unit, and let the water run through till the end. Then turn off the unit. Put several cut-up lemons into the disposal, put the stopper in the sink, and fill to the top with water again. Remove the stopper, turn the unit on, and run until it runs smooth. That should take care of all of the odors. Always use cold water in your disposal; if there are any bits of grease in the unit, cold water is more likely to carry them away. Here's another little tip: every once in a while dump a tray of ice cubes into the sink, while the water is running This will help to dislodge pieces of food that were not removed the first time. It will also help to keep your blades sharp.

E

Enamel: Enamel can scratch very easily, so don't use anything abrasive on the surface. Wipe down with warm, soapy water. If the enamel piece is your stove top and there are bits stuck to the top, fill a pot with water, bring it to the boil, use that water to soften whatever has hardened onto the surface, then wipe it away. This goes for under the top too. Remember; do not use anything abrasive on enamel. Another little tip: dissolve a tablespoon of powdered detergent in warm water; then use this to wipe down the stove top. Rinse it clean, and dry.

F

Formica: Formica is a plastic laminate. It's very easy to keep clean. Use warm, soapy water. If there is a stain on the surface, mix some baking soda and water into a paste, and apply to the stain. Let it stand for a few minutes; then wash off.

Gelcoat is sold at hardware stores. It will restore your Formica surface by hiding scratches and adding a shine back into the laminate.

Fruit fly: The fruit fly comes into the home in August, when all of the fruit has ripened and contains the most sugar. These flies will not bite. You can get rid of them very easily by taking a jar, adding some cider vinegar, and placing a paper cone into the opening. The flies will be attracted to the cider and will climb in, but they will not be able to get back out. Just flush them away, and you're done.

G

Gold: Put boiling water and squirt of liquid detergent into a small container. Add your gold item, and any dirt or grime will disappear almost immediately. Use a toothbrush for nooks and crannies, if necessary; it won't hurt anything.

Granite: The easiest way to clean granite is to use warm, soapy water followed by a clean-water rinse. There are plenty of cleaners with chemicals in them, but I would stay away from them, particularly if you prepare food on granite counters. Remember to keep it simple. Every year or two have a professional reseal your counters, and you should be just fine. Avoid creating stains by using a trivet for your food.

Here's a great tip to pass on to your friends: for hard-to-remove stains caused by marker pens, use some acetone on a rag. To remove wine stains that will not come out, in a small bowl add 1 cup of plaster along with some bleach to make it into a paste. Spread it over the stain and let stand for about thirty to forty minutes. Then take a sponge with water and remove the plaster. The stain should be gone. If not repeat the process.

Grease: Enzymes in the form of powdered detergents are the number one cleaner for this job. Dissolve quarter cup of powdered detergent in hot water, wet a rag, and wipe the grease off. Rinse the item with hot water and dry. If the grease is hard, put some detergent on it, wet a rag completely with hot water, and put it on the grease spot for about a half hour to soften. Then rinse out the rag, wipe down the spot, and dry.

L

Leather: Finished leather can be cleaned by taking a mild soap like Ivory or Dove and working it into lather. With a clean, damp towel, wipe off the soap bubbles; then polish with a dry towel. Add a conditioner at the end; leather honey is the best I've found (www.leatherhoney.com).

For unfinished leather, use saddle soap. Work it into lather; then wipe it off. Let it air dry; then use mink oil (available from www.amazon.com) to condition the object.

Limestone: Because limestone is so porous and soft, it needs a penetrating sealer. Stone Technologies, Corp. (www.stonetechnologiesinc.com) has one of the best products on the market, available in various quantities.

Stone Soap Ultra is a pH-controlled product made for cleaning stone. This is not a spray-and-wipe cleaner. Dilute this product in water, and wash your floor. It will not leave a residue, keep all citrus products away from your limestone they. Will stain your stone.

M

Marble: Stone Soap Ultra from Stone Technologies, Corp. (www.stonetechnologiesinc.com) is the best cleaner for marble, and all other stone products. A product listed as Sealer #2 is ideal for marble.

Microwaves: Fill a bowl with water and the juice of one lemon. Put the bowl into the microwave, and turn on high for five minutes—until steaming occurs—then let it sit for another two to three minutes to penetrate any baked on items. Open the door, and wipe down the inside. The lemon will make it smell great. If necessary, repeat the process to remove any baked-on mess that did not come off. Then repeat and wipe as before.

Mice: Of course the first thing we think to do when we see a mouse is to buy mousetraps and set them around the house. If you see a mouse, measure a ten-foot distance from where you saw it, and that will probably be where the mice are nesting. By setting traps with some peanut butter and distributing them around the area, you should be able to get rid of them. You can also buy bait containers from d-CON (www.d-conproducts.com) and place them around the area. Both will work very well.

Moldings:
1. Using a paint brush works just fine. It will get into all of the crevices.
2. Another option is to use a bucket with warm water and with a few drops of liquid soap. Dip your microfiber cloth in the water, wring it out, and wipe down the moldings. Dry with a soft towel if necessary.

O

Onyx:
1. Once again, Stone Soap Ultra is the cleaner you want, because of its low pH levels and lack of abrasives. To order, go to www.stonetechnologiesinc.com.
2. Warm, soapy water, applied with a very soft rag, also will do just fine. Use a minimum of soap. Chances are your onyx item is sealed, so cleaning this way will not hurt it at all. Wipe down with a soft towel.

Oven: This is a two-step process. First, use Easy-Off to clean your oven. The great thing is that this product is almost totally fume free. Take out the racks, spray the inside of the oven, and wait a few hours; even better, wait overnight. Put the racks on some newspaper, spray them too, and wait overnight. Easy-Off also makes a cleaner for self-cleaning ovens; remember to take out the racks, or their shine may burn off.

Second, dissolve some powdered detergent in a bucket of hot water; wet a sponge with scratch pad. Use gloves if you need to. Wipe down the inside of the oven with the scratch side of the sponge. Once everything has been wiped down, rinse with clear water. Now look for any spots that have hardened.

Use either the Easy-Off spray or a razor-blade scraper to remove the remaining spots. Then, rinse; the oven should look like new. Take the racks to the sink, and wipe them down with the sponge and some hot water. If the racks still have spots, use a zero grade steel-wool to help them disappear.

Another option for cleaning ovens is Bio Green Clean. Follow directions on the bottle. Spray the oven and racks, using a 3:1 ratio. All of those little enzymes will start munching on the oven and its racks, and soon it will look like new. Wipe down with hot water, using your sponge with the scratch pad. If the oven still has some hardened spots, use the razor-blade scraper to remove them. When we can work chemically free it's a very good idea.

P

Pet stains: Bio Green Clean is my all-time favorite product for removing pet stains and odors. It's a miracle worker, filled with enzymes that munch their way right through your stains and leave your house odor free. Follow the easy directions on the bottle, and all of your worries will soon be gone. To find other products, go to www.petstainoff.com a site dedicated to the removal of pet stains.

Porcelain: I use Lysol disinfectant liquid on all porcelain tiles. Add a half cup of the disinfectant to a bucket of warm water, wet your microfiber cloth, and start washing the floor. To clean spots, add water to a little scouring powder to make it into slurry. Using a stiff brush, scrub over the spots until they are gone. Rinse well, and wipe dry with a towel.

Because each spill or spot will require a different cleaning process, go to www.porcelainenamel.com for suggestions about how to handle. Remember that porcelain enamel appliances and fixtures are recyclable; for more information, call 1-800-937-1226. To speak to someone about recycling your porcelain.

R

Refrigerator: Put on your gloves; you'll need them for this job. Fill a bucket with hot water; add one cup of bleach. I usually remove one shelf at a time, taking off all items before then removing the shelf itself. Put each shelf in the sink; have the bucket of hot water and bleach nearby. Run the hot water in the sink, dip a sponge into the bucket, and start wiping down the shelf. The bleach will remove all of the spills and disinfect the surface at the same time. Once the shelf is clean, rinse and dry it. Before you return it to the refrigerator, wipe the walls, all the way down to the next shelf. Return the shelf to the fridge. Wipe all items that you return to the fridge. That means running them under water and wiping them clean. Repeat this process until you reach the bottom of the fridge where the drawers are located. Remove the drawers and the products in them. Wash the drawers in the sink using the bleach mixture, and rinse when done. Once the box has been cleaned, move on to the door shelves. If they are removable then Remove them one by one, taking off all of the items from each shelf. Wash the shelves with the bleach mixture, and then rinse. Wipe down the door panel as far down to the next shelf. Then rinse and dry each item before returning it to the shelf.

To clean the freezer, use the same process. Fill a bucket with hot water and bleach. With a freestanding freezer, remove each shelf, one at a time, wash the shelves in the sink, rinse, then wipe off freezer walls down to the next shelf. Return items to the freezer. To clean the box on top of the fridge, remove everything. Take the hot water and bleach mixture, and wipe out the box. If there are stains, use more hot water and some bleach on a rag, and wipe until they are gone. Return all items to the freezer. Of course, this is a great time to get rid of things that you no longer need or want, like expired items. When you are done, wipe down the outside of the refrigerator—the whole thing: front, sides, and back. Roll it out to get at the back. Clean the walls around the refrigerator as well as the floor beneath. Roll it back into place, and enjoy your clean fridge.

Roaches: They've survived nuclear blasts, so what makes us think we can get rid of them? However, even if we can't get rid of them, we can make a really good run at them by setting down sticky sheets that will trap them so they cannot move. Baiting them is probably the best. Find a good exterminator and ask them to mix up a batch of bait that will harden like candy. You can take the mixture and have it placed under the counter at baseboard level, under sinks, etc. Once the bait has hardened, the roaches will lick it, ingest it into themselves, and take it back to their nests. It will then kill all of the babies and anything else that wants to lick it. I used this treatment once in an apartment building that I owned, and they were gone within a week. Remember, feeding them is best. If you are infested with large numbers, you may want to bomb the place. Open your cabinets, place some paper on a chair, and place the bomb on top, close all of the windows. Pull the tab on the top, leave the house for a few hours, and when you return, open all of the windows to air the house out for a few more hours. This can be messy, and it requires that you absolutely wash everything down afterward.

Rust: Rust Off is the best product I've ever seen. Simply spray, and watch the rust disappear. Get it at www.wash-safe.com.

S

Shades: Fill a spray bottle with warm water, add a couple drops of Ivory liquid soap, and shake the bottle. Pull down the shade, and spray it with the liquid soap. Wipe down with a microfiber cloth, and dry with a clean dry towel. If the shades are stained with heavy marks, put some baking soda on a damp rag and wipe over the area until the marks are gone. Rinse with clear water, and dry.

Silver: Baking soda is a great cleaner. I've used it on my silver for years. It is nonabrasive and brings the shine right back to your pieces. Pour one cup of baking soda in a bowl, wet a microfiber cloth with hot water, dip it into the baking soda, and start rubbing your silver. It will become clean very fast. For hard-to-reach areas, use a soft toothbrush, rub vigorously, and rinse. Dry with a clean towel.

Handle silver chains slightly differently. Line a bowl with aluminum foil. Add your chains, cover them with baking soda, pour boiling water over them, and use a spoon or brush to move them around in the mixture. Remove them from the bowl, and rinse and dry them off. If they are in really bad shape, you may need to repeat this process several times.

Here is a list of websites for good products with a tarnishing shield that can help keep your silver longer:

www.tarnishield.com

www.weiman.com

Twinkle and Goddards can be found at www. amazon.com.goddards is a gel paste for cleaning silver and can be found in some grocery stores.

Silverfish: Silverfish are insects that do not bite, but they will eat paper crumbs on the floor, etc. If you are infested, take some cloves and place them around the areas that you see the silverfish. They will go away permanently because they do not like the smell. You can help yourself by keeping the area free of food and water.

Stainless steel: There is any number of sprays available for cleaning stainless-steel appliances; once again, however, simplicity is the aim.

First wipe down the appliance with a warm, soapy solution to remove all attached material. Then add a few drops of baby oil—that's right, baby oil—to a paper towel. Rub the stainless steel clean, taking off all marks. Then use a dry paper towel to remove the excess oil until the appliance is dry and shiny

If your stainless steel has marks or spots that needs to be removed, use a mixture of baking soda and a lemon or a lime. Dip half of a lemon or lime into the baking soda; then rub in circles over the surface until the spots have been removed. Rinse thoroughly, and dry with a clean towel.

Here are a couple of methods that I've used over the years. Use window cleaner on your stainless-steel refrigerator. It removes the finger prints and shines at the same time. For the sink, I use a regular bar of soap. Wet a microfiber cloth; rub the soap over it to create a good lather; then rub the stainless with the cloth until the entire sink has a smooth surface. Rinse and dry. Your sink should look new. Add some baby oil to a dry cloth, and rub over the sink for a great shine. Dry thoroughly. I'll bet you'll be able to see yourself in the shine.

T

Tar: There is an all-natural product made from citrus that removes tar in one easy process. Just spray, and rinse off with clear water. Mix according to directions. To order, go to www.interstateproducts. com. Here's a helpful hint I learned as a young boy on the farm: put some gasoline on a rag, and wipe off the tar. How easy could that be? Rinse with warm, soapy water and dry.

Tin: Keeping tin free from dust and stains is a must. Use warm, soapy water, and then dry with a clean towel. If there is rust, sprinkle some Bar Keepers Friend (www.barkeepersfriend.com) on the spot, and scrub with a wet rag until the rust is gone. Then rinse and dry. Use a metal polish like Brasso to finish the job.

W

Wallpaper: Brush your walls to remove any dust, cobwebs, etc. Fill a bucket with warm water, and add about one squirt of liquid detergent. Agitate the water to get the bubbles started, and dunk your sponge. Place towels at the bottom of the wall to catch any drips or spills. Wring out the sponge, and start wiping at the top of the wall, working your way to the bottom. I know this sounds contrary to what I've already told you about washing walls, but wallpaper is a different animal and needs to be cleaned from top to bottom. This should be enough to dry the wall, but sometimes you'll need a towel to go over it. Move onto the next section, and work your way around the room until you are done.

Generally, wallpaper in bath and kitchen is coated with vinyl and will not be harmed if water and cleansers are applied in small amounts. If the bathroom has some mold spots, use a solution of warm water and a small amount of bleach. This will remove the mold and disinfect at the same time. In the kitchen, use the trusty standby, a powdered detergent, so the enzymes can munch their way through any grease that has attached itself to the walls.

Walls: Start by dusting your walls. If you don't have a wall duster, then use a foxtail brush. If that doesn't work, get out the vacuum cleaner, attach the brush to the hose, and vacuum the walls from top to bottom.

Get two buckets. Fill one with about a gallon of warm water. Fill the other one about three-quarters full. To bucket number one, add a cup of vinegar, a cup of ammonia, and a quarter cup of baking soda. Put on your gloves, and drop a sponge in each bucket. Put towels at the wall baseboards and start washing your walls in sections, from bottom to top. After each section, rinse, then move onto the next section. Continue around the room until you have finished. Be sure to wash the baseboards and trim, including around the doors. If there are marks like crayon on the walls, use a blow dryer to melt the wax, and wipe it off with a damp rag. To clean marks from shoes or luggage, put some toothpaste on a rag and scrub them clean. Rinse when finished, and move onto the next room.

Washer and dryer: Yes, they need to be cleaned. Fill a bucket with warm water, and add a squirt of liquid detergent. Wet your microfiber cloth, and wipe down the outsides of both machines.

Remove the lint basket from the dryer. Add the piece with the small hole in the end to the vacuum cleaner, and vacuum the lint basket container. Pull as much of the lint free from the inside as possible. It's important to have the dryer hose professionally cleaned at least once a year. If it's plugged, it can cause a fire. Also vacuum behind the dryer and underneath if possible.

If your washing machine has an agitator, remove the top piece, and clean out the buildup of gunk from liquid detergent that accumulates there. Usually hot water and a very fine brush will dislodge any buildup. Over time, if this is not done, your machine will have to work twice as hard to clean your clothes. Owners of newer washers, which do not have agitators, do not need to go through this process.

Windows: Fill a spray bottle with warm water, and add about five drops of liquid detergent. Spray your window, and then use a soft brush to scrub it clean. Remove excess spray with a squeegee (www. bettymills.com), and wipe the edges with a dry cloth.

Wood: Some Murphy's Flax Oil Soap in a bucket of warm water works just fine on finished wood. Pledge will work and leave the surface looking like glass.

Harrell's (www.thefurnitureconnoisseur.com) is a wax used for antiques and the finest wood furniture. Use a very soft rag, such as a T-shirt or, better yet, a baby blanket. Apply the wax, and work it in to the wood. Let it stand for a while; then use another baby blanket to polish it to a shine.

If you have high-end antiques, you will probably hire a professional to polish and wax your furniture every six months. All professionals use their own mixtures. Be sure to ask what they will use to finish your furniture. I used to work with someone who used a French method to polish wood and leather: the ash from Mount St. Helen's along with his own liquid infusion. When he finished working on a leather item, I could clearly see my face. Dusting antique wood should be done with baby blankets only, as this ensures the finish will remain on the wood.

Beeswax (www.beepolish) is a standard wax for all types of wood furniture. I've used it for years. It comes in several forms and is used by rubbing into your wood with the grain. Over time, your wood will feel like silk.

Wrought iron: Wipe clean with a dry towel. Use some steel wool and a couple drops of turpentine to remove rust. Then apply a coat of wax to keep the rust from coming back.

Cleaning Product Links—
Hitting the Bull's-Eye

www.amazon.com
To order Twinkle for silver, copper, and brass
(Also S.O.S. and mink oil)

www.limeaway.com
To clean lime from sinks, tubs, and showers

www.leatherhoney.com
For cleaning leather furniture and more

www.stonetechnologiesinc.com
To clean stone, onyx, and marble

www.d-conproducts.com
To help rid ants, roaches, and mice

www.petstainoff.com
For removal of pet stains

www.porcelainenamel.com
To clean porcelain

www.wash-safe.com
For cleaning rust off

www.armandhammer.com
To order baking soda to clean silver, to deodorize the
refrigerator, and to use in your sinks' pipes

www.weiman.com
To clean silver

www.interstateproducts.com
For cleaning out tar

www.barkeepersfriend.com
For cleaning tin or hard-to-remove, baked-on grease

www.bettymills.com
To order a squeegee or other janitorial supplies

www.colgate.com
To order Murphy's Oil Soap for fine woods

www.pledge.com
For cleaning wood, granite, and glass

www.thefurnitureconnoisseur.com
To order Harrell's Wax for fine furniture

www.beepolish.com
For fine woods of all kinds

www.containerstore.com
For every size container you can think of and then some

www.biogreenclean.com
To order cleaners for all purposes (plant-based)

www.artinstituteof Chicago.com
For information on cleaning all manner of art, from oils and marbles and bronzes to historic art pieces, including furniture

www.easyoff.us
For cleaning your oven

www.lovittblinds.com
For cleaning your blinds the ultra-sound way

www.amazon.com
For brass polish
(Just search for Brasso, one of the best)

www.autogeek.net
To order the metal cleaner Wenol for brass

The Master Bedroom—
The First Hurdle

The first thing to do when cleaning the master bedroom is turn on the lights. Open your window treatments, and let the fresh air in. Then look around the room and remove any cobwebs.

Then turn your attention to anything hanging about the room: clothes that need to be hung or sent to the laundry, shoes that need to be returned to their place in the closet, and any articles on top of dressers, side tables, and headboard platforms.

Look for papers that need to be put in the trash can or a nearby drawer or cabinet shelf. Place all CDs and DVDs where they belong; that goes for the remotes as well. There's one more task to do before we get started and that is to make the bed; change the sheets if you need to. Once the bed has been returned to its former glory, fluff and arrange the pillows.

Fill a bucket with water, wet and wring out a microfiber cloth, and start dusting all of the furniture in the room. Start on one side, and work your way around the whole room until everything has been dusted. This includes all of the drawer fronts and handles and all of the multimedia, including the computer, if it is in this room.

Next turn your attention to any artworks. Use a dry cloth on oil paintings; if your artwork is under glass, wipe it down with a damp cloth. Do the same for family photos. Then look at the tops of the cabinets. If you have pieces that need special care, like crystal, wash them and make them sparkle. About the only thing you will not do is pick up the bed and dust underneath it, but that's for another day. Now move out of the room; you're done. Don't worry about vacuuming if you have carpets as that will be accomplished once the whole house is clean. You'll be doing too much walking about right now. If you have wood floors, however, by all means mop them now. Follow the recommendations from the floor's manufacturer, or use my cleaner: some water mixed with Lysol in a bucket. Use a mop, or better yet get down on your hands and knees. Either way, the room will look and smell great.

Before moving on to the next bedroom, the teenager's room, you may want to put a padlock on the door and keep going. But let's brave it and head in, at least for the experience. Put on your boots; here we go.

The Teenager's Bedroom— Into the Deep End

Empty and refill your bucket, move past the "keep out" sign, and enter your teenager's room at your own risk. Turn on the lights; then open the window treatments and windows, and let in some fresh air. Put all trash into garbage bags. Pick up all of the clothing that needs to be washed and put it into a new bag. Hang anything that should be hung, and put any clothing that needs to go to the dry cleaners into another bag so you can take it there. Next, move to the bed itself; strip it of all bedding, and take anything that needs to be washed to the laundry room. Remove anything that is underneath the bed. Make the bed: add clean sheets, comforters, pillows, and maybe even some stuffed animals.if they are still into them.

I remember working for a family many years ago on the outskirts of the city. There were three sons. One was immaculate—everything was in its place, the bed was always made, and there was never anything on the floor.

Everything was neatly hung in the closet. Another son, the oldest, was very messy, but his room was easily put back into order. The third son, the youngest of the three, was on another planet. I knew when I walked into his room that I would be there for quite some time. Nothing was put away, and there were clothes strewn all about the room as well as all over the closet floor. His mother asked me what could be done to help him get the room into order and I told her it was time to take action and let him know that his behavior was unacceptable. So I came up with a system to get him put into order. The very next week, everything that was not put away went into bags, and the bags were put on top of his bed. He was told that whatever items he wanted to keep needed to be put away wherever they belonged, or next week they would disappear. Of course he chose to press the issue, and his mother asked what we could do. I politely told her it was time to go to the next step and take everything down to the garage and put the bags next to the trash cans. When he came home and couldn't find his things, he asked his mother where they were. She let him know that they were in the garage and that if he wanted them he should take them upstairs and put everything away, or the next step would be to take them out with the trash, never to return—and nothing would be replaced, either. After that little lesson, all of the boys did what they were told, and their rooms were, for the most part, in order when I arrived. The boys' mother was very pleased with the outcome, and I was then asked to repeat that little lesson in some of their friends' homes. Be honest with your kids. If you let them know you mean what you say and do, they will follow your lead. Moving on.

Remove anything on the tops of dressers, side tables, media centers, and computers and wipe them down. Put away all papers that do not need to be out. You'll figure this out as you go along, and adjust accordingly. Finally, wash down the room. Start on one side and work your way around the room, remembering to look up to find and remove cobwebs as you go. Wipe down everything in sight: all trophies, knickknacks, photos and books etc.. If the water in the bucket is dirty, change it and continue. Wipe down any mirrors in the room. If books need to be straightened, do so. If pictures are on the walls, clean them. This would also be a good time to wash the window exteriors, if it is at all possible. If not, just wash the insides and do the outsides another time. Straighten up the closet if necessary.

If the floors are wood, now is the time to clean them. You may want to vacuum first and then wash them. Fill the bucket with warm water and some Lysol (or whatever the floor manufacturer recommends), and use a mop or get down on your knees. If you have carpets, wait until you've finished cleaning the entire house to vacuum. If it's still light out and you're not too traumatized by this experience, move to the third and last bedroom. Let's call this the baby's room.

The Baby's Room—
A Clean Sweep

Change the water in the bucket, and add the Lysol cleaner. Turn on the lights and open the window treatments. When the fresh air is pouring in, you'll be ready to clean the baby's room.

Start by looking for and removing cobwebs. Pick up anything that has found its way onto the floor, and put those articles back where they belong. Change the sheets and blankets to the babies bed when necessary. Empty diaper containers and any other receptacles.

Wipe down the entire room: changing table, crib, bookcases, toy boxes, etc. By now you know the drill: wipe absolutely everything, including knickknacks, books, multimedia, lamps, etc. Straighten up the closet, if necessary. After everything has been wiped down, wash the windows. Then turn your attention to the floor. If your floors are carpeted, wait until you have finished cleaning the house to vacuum. But if you have wooden floors, go ahead and vacuum them now. Then wash them. Fill the bucket with warm water, and pour in about a half cup of the Lysol cleaner. Use a mop or get down on your hands and knees with a rag, and clean the floor. The room is sure to looks and smells great.

The Bathroom—
A Fresh Start

No matter how big your bathroom is, it is important to keep it spotless. Turn on the lights, and let's get moving. You may want to turn on the radio here.

The first step is to remove all items that will get in the way of cleaning, such as everything on top of the vanity or toilet. Also remove the towels hanging from hooks or in the shower, the trash container, and any throw rugs on the floor. If your tub or shower is loaded with bottles, kid's toys, brushes, soap, and so on, remove them. Now that you have a clean palette, you can start to clean.

Look up; if you need to remove cobwebs, do it now. Fill the sink with warm water, and put in a tablespoon of powdered detergent. Dissolve the detergent, and soak your microfiber cloth. Wring out the cloth well, and wipe down any wall-mounted lighting fixtures. If the wall above the sink is all mirror, then spray window cleaner over it; take the wet microfiber cloth and wipe it down. Then go over it with your squeegee. The mirror should sparkle, with no streaks. Add some water to the sink again, and dissolve some of the powdered detergent in it. Wet and wring out the microfiber cloth. Then use the damp cloth to wipe down the front and sides of the vanity. Make sure to clean the vanity handles or knobs. Turn your attention to the top of the vanity and the sink. Add some fresh water in the sink, add a tablespoon of powdered detergent and dissolve it in the sink along with adding the micro cloth then use this liquid to wash down the sink and vanity top. Dry with a towel.

Now move to the toilet. Flush first. Then add some of the Lysol liquid—not a lot; it goes a long way. Put on your gloves, and dive into the bowl with the microfiber cloth. Create bubbles in the bowl by shaking your hand, then take the cloth and wipe down the toilet from top to bottom, inside and out. Once all the nook and crannies are washed, wring out the cloth, and wipe down the toilet from top to bottom. Flush again, and you're done. set the cloth aside and don't use again until it has been laundered .

Move on to the tub. If your tub is surrounded by tile, fill the bucket with some water, add one or two tablespoons of the powdered detergent, and dunk your microfiber cloth into the water so that it is totally wet. Then wet the walls around the tub. You may need to get right into the tub to accomplish this, so hop in. it's much easier if you do.

There are several things you can do at this point, but I'll concentrate on one and talk about the others later. Dip your sponge with scratch pad attached into the water. Scrub all of the walls and when you are finished, wipe the fixtures with the wet microfiber cloth. Fill the cup with hot water, and rinse the walls and fixtures. Remove yourself from the tub. Kneel next to the tub, put in the stopper, and turn on the hot water, add enough to cover half of the bottom. . Dissolve a couple of tablespoons of powdered detergent in the water; then use the sponge with scrubber to clean the tub from top to bottom. If your tub has a surface that scratches easily, use the microfiber cloth to perform this task. Open the stopper, and rinse the tub with warm water. At this point, you'll be done, unless a ring has reappeared around the tub. If so, put some more hot water in the bottom of the tub, wet the sponge, sprinkle some of the powdered detergent on the scrubber, and work your way around the tub. That should do it. Rinse the tub again, and move onto the shower, if it is separate unit.

If the shower has a handheld sprayer, then spray the entire inside of the shower to get it wet. As before, fill the bucket with some hot water, the hotter the better, dissolve some powdered detergent in it, wet the sponge and use it to scrub the walls from top to bottom. Include the doors to the shower and the tracks to the doors. Then rinse the walls and doors, and move onto the floor. Using the scratch side of the sponge, go over the floor; if you need more detergent, add it to the wet floor and scrub with the sponge. Rinse. You're done. Oops, not quite yet.

It's time to return all the items that you removed. Start by folding the towels and setting them aside. If you keep shampoo bottles in the tub or shower, wet the microfiber cloth, wipe the bottles clean, and return them to their original positions. The same goes for the kid's toys; wash and return them. Your vanity is next: wash and return everything you removed. Now, you're done. Well, not quite; fooled you again!

Here's a little trick. Take your tilex cleaner and spray the bottom of the shower and anywhere you see black dots, which are mold. Spray around the tub as well. Next, move to the floor. Fill the bucket with warm water and add some Lysol. Wet a microfiber cloth, and clean the floor. If the floor is very dirty, let the cloth sit for a few seconds; then take your brush and scrub the floor. Wring out the cloth, and wipe up the water. Move onto the next section, and repeat until you have worked your way out of the room. Return the towels to their positions and the rug to the floor. Here's a little hint: At the beginning of the cleaning session, put the towels in the dryer, and run it until they are all dry. This is done to refresh the towels then return them to the bathroom. Then you will be done, and I'll bet the bathroom will look great. Good work.

Every house has a rhythm. Find the rhythm for your home. Every time you clean, use the same routine. For example, if you have a two-story home, you may want to start upstairs, and then move downstairs, or vice versa, whichever is more comfortable for you. Over the years, I have found that it's best to get the rhythm right from the get-go, and then stick with it. That way you know you've cleaned your whole home, and can always add things later, like vacuuming all the furniture or cleaning the windows.

The Living Room— Keeping the Pace

Just as cleaning the bathroom and bedrooms had its own rhythm, so does the living room. We use this room for conversation and entertaining, and just as in rowing, everyone should be moving in the same direction. Turn on the lights, and take a good look around. Look up; if you see any cobwebs, remove them. Open the window treatments and the windows, and let in the fresh air. Look around the room to see if anything is out of place. When you are satisfied that all is well, start by straightening the room: make sure the cushions on the couch are aligned and that the backs are straight and fluffed. If you have books or magazines on a table, arrange them neatly. If art is hanging on the walls, straighten it as needed. If you use this room a lot, it may contain items that don't belong; remove them.

Fill up the bucket with warm water and add some of the powdered detergent. Wet a microfiber cloth, and wipe down everything that you see in the room. If there is glass, use your glass cleaner; if there are mirrors, the same applies. If you have cabinetry filled with crystal or shelves lined with books, make sure they are cleaned as well.

This is the room that most people see when they enter your home, so make it shine. Be sure to wash the windows, and of course if your floors are wood, clean them now as well. Vacuum them if necessary, and then mop or wash them. If you have carpets, wait until you have cleaned the entire house to vacuum.

When you think you are done, go back and look around. Put any misplaced items back where they belong; if the crystal and glass are not sparkling, clean them again. In other words, make sure this room shines and keep it that way. It will make your life a lot easier. Now, let's move on to the dining room.

The Dining Room—
Our Second Wind

The dining room is a very special place, used for all types of occasions, particularly grand ones. This is another room that will be seen by most guests to the house, so it needs special care.

Omit nothing when cleaning the dining room, and this means from top to bottom. No one wants to eat in a space that has so much dust the meal is not noticed, and the conversation is lost as well.

The first thing to do is to turn on the lights. Take down any cobwebs; then turn your attention to the light fixture hanging above the table. If you can wipe it with a dry cloth, use a microfiber cloth. If it is made of glass, wash it. (Turn off the power to the fixture before using any liquid.) If it is crystal, wipe each piece. If there are shades on your fixture, wipe them clean. You get the picture. Make it shine; it is the centerpiece of the room.

Get ready to do some real work in the dining room. Side hutches usually have glass doors, cabinetry, and shelves. Piece by piece, remove all the items inside, and take them to the kitchen. Put down some towels on the kitchen counter. Wet a microfiber cloth, add a little liquid detergent, and make the cloth very soapy. Piece by piece, wash each item from the hutch with the cloth; then rinse it in warm water and place on the towels to dry. Go back into the dining room, and wipe down the first shelf, top and bottom, all sides, and the glass on the doors. When the glass is sparkling, return the pieces in the kitchen to their rightful places, move on to the next shelf, and repeat the process until the entire hutch has been cleaned.

If you have a sideboard, wipe down the exterior, and then treat any pieces resting on the top the same way you treated the ones in the hutch. If your sideboard has silver, put it aside and clean it at the end.

Move onto the table and chairs. Wipe down the top of the table, the sides, and then the legs or pedestals. Wipe down each chair entirely. Wipe the bottom of the hutch if you didn't do it earlier. Sometimes there is other furniture in the room, and now is the time to wipe it down as well. If you have furniture made of fine wood, use wax or polish to clean it and make it shine. Make sure all of the surfaces are completely dry after you use these products. Then turn your attention to the covers on the chairs, either vacuuming them or wiping them clean with a dry microfiber cloth. Does it look good?

Clean your windows now. Then clean your wooden floors. If the room is carpeted, wait until you've cleaned the rest of the house. Don't forget about the silver. Clean those pieces, and return them to their places on the sideboard. Clean the centerpiece on the table and the wall sconces. Make sure the art hanging on the walls has been cleaned .

You are officially ready for any occasion that will bring family and friends together to celebrate. Enjoy the room.

The Family Room— The Last Hurdle

How's that rhythm going? If you have the music on, I'll bet everything is just fine. Every house has a playroom, a place where all of the multimedia is located, where you root for your favorite team, and where you serve food to your guests while you watch the game. Just as with the pentathlon, this room is multifunctional. This is the family room.

Of course, turn on the lights first. Look for those telltale signs that spiders have visited, and if they have taken up residence, evict them. Then open the window treatments, and let in the fresh air. Dissolve some powdered detergent in a bucket of warm water. Add a few microfiber cloths to the bucket, and move into the family room. You're almost ready to start wiping down the room, but first straighten it up. Remove anything that can be taken away, such as books newspapers, food, or empty glasses. This is also a good time to put bookcases in order by lining up the titles. Put artworks and photographs in their designated places, and fluff and straighten the sofa and chair cushions. Rearrange the side pillows, and your mother's Afghans, if you have them. Get everything that does not belong there off the floor, and return it to its rightful place. If the room has a fireplace, check the flue vent, and make sure it is in the appropriate position, if you have trees in this room, shake them to remove all of the dead leaves. Check the vases of live flowers, and change or add water if necessary.

Take a good look at the room, and make sure it's in order. Wet your first microfiber cloth, and wring it dry. Start on one side of the room, and work your way around the room, wiping everything. Don't leave anything out, including the tables and chairs, lamps, sconces, mantle and wall around the fireplace, built-in or other shelves that hold books, CDs, and DVDs. Use a dry microfiber cloth to wipe down multimedia units or computers as you don't want to get these items wet. To wipe down the keyboard and mouse, however, you can use a damp cloth that has hardly any moisture left in it. Take crystal pieces to the kitchen to be cleaned, just as you did in the dining room.

Look to the walls, and wipe down any artworks. Use a dry microfiber cloth for oils, and wipe anything under glass with a damp cloth. Be sure to wipe down the frames of all the artwork; if you are going to go to the trouble of cleaning it, clean all of it. No one wants to look at dust surrounding a great work of art. Then, clean your windows.

There may be a piano in this room. If so, never use a dry rag on the piano. It can scratch the finish. Instead use a feather duster or a damp rag that has been put into filtered water. The filtering will remove the minerals which can alter the finish. Don't use paper towels make sure the rags are very soft. I like using a baby blanket. Stay away from cleaning any of the interior parts, leave that for the professionals.

If this room has a wet or dry bar, also wipe that area down. All bottles, glassware, mirrors, shelving, and cabinetry should be spotless when you are done.

Turn your attention to the floors. If they are made of wood, vacuum them. Change the water in the bucket; by now, you will have done that task several times in this room. Fill the bucket up halfway, dissolve some of the powdered detergent, and add the microfiber cloths. Once again, use a kneepad and get down on the floor to wash it, or use a mop. Take the time to wipe the baseboards as you go; this will save a lot of grief later, when you look down and see the dust hanging off the boards.

As you are cleaning, it's important to take the time to look at the room as you go. Spend the time to rearrange items, and make the room photo-ready. Strive for this. Look at books and magazines to get ideas for arranging your furniture and placing your artworks. It doesn't matter what is displayed on your walls or tables; they all have their rightful places. Your job is to put them there, and keep them clean.

Well, we've arrived at the end of another room. The windows are open, the fresh air is pouring in, and the house smells great.

The Laundry Room—
Cycling through to the End

These days, a laundry room might be a stackable unit in a closet or an upstairs hallway or bathroom. Perhaps your washer and dryer are in their own room or the basement. Wherever you do your laundry, the space needs to be clean and orderly at all times; otherwise, how will you know where anything is? You wash, dry, fold, and then return your clothes to their rightful place. Thank goodness for whoever invented these machines to do the work for us, or we would all be pounding our clothes on a rock in some stream.

Of course by now you've learned to turn on the lights, and have a good look around the room. Get started by.

Removing anything that does not belong. There may be baskets filled with laundry, an ironing board, or cleansers on the floor next to the machine, particularly if there is no closet in the room. One of my clients keeps empty shopping bags alongside her washer, just in case she needs them. Whatever the case is, remove everything from the floor or alongside of your machines. Vacuum behind the washer and dryer, if necessary. Fill the bucket with warm water and add some powdered detergent; then wipe down everything in the room. Always start at the top of the room. Remove the cob-webs and dust the walls if necessary. Clean the cabinets, then the machines, and the laundry tub, if you have one. Wipe down the closet doors, their handles or pulls, the door to the room itself, and the window.

Change the water and put some of the powdered detergent in the bucket, add the microfiber cloths, and move onto the floor. Whether you get down on your knees or use a mop, make this floor shine. When you're finished, put back everything you removed: cleaning bottles, baskets, ironing board, trash can, etc., change out the water in your bucket and lets move to the entry.

The Entryway—
First Impressions

The entryway is the space that will be seen by everyone entering your home, so make sure that it is kept in order at all times. Whether it opens right into the living room or into a stairwell, this space should be kept spotless. As they say, first impressions make lasting impressions, so don't leave shoes lying about on the floor. Pick them up, and put them where they belong. If you have a display case or shelf that hangs on the wall, make sure it holds only decorative items. Keep benches, chairs, or stools clear. They are not places for throwing coats; that's what the closet is for. The goal is to clear the entryway of all items that do not belong there so that cleaning can begin.

Turn on the lights. Look for spiders to see if they have left anything behind. If they have, remove those cobwebs, and focus on the light fixture, perhaps a chandelier, a hanging lantern, or recessed lighting. Whatever the case, clean it all and make it shine.

Fill the bucket with warm water and some Lysol liquid; add the microfiber cloths, and you'll be ready to go. Wipe everything down, including all of the furniture, mirrors, and the art on the walls. Wipe down all of the doors as well, including the handles they are often the place where germs reside. Then take a look around. Ensure that everything is in its rightful place; then change the water in the bucket and mop the floor. Make sure to wipe down the baseboards as you go. Whether your home has a floor made of marble, onyx, wood, tile, or stone, find out what type of cleaner is needed before cleaning the floor.

If the entryway has a staircase, wipe that down too from the top of the rail to the spindles and treads. — If the stairs do not have a runner, make sure they are spotless too. If there is a runner, then wait until you vacuum the entire house.

The Kitchen—
Crossing the Finish Line

This room seems to stop most people from doing any cleaning in their home. This is the triathlon of your home. You will need all of your stamina to get to the end. If the thought of it bores you, turn on some music or the TV for background noise. Music works very well for me.

Turn on the lights. Remove everything from the counters. Put it all away where it belongs, and keep it there until you need it. Put all trash in the bin; separate it if you recycle. Move anything attached to your refrigerator to a basket. Either put the basket away, or plan to return your items to the fridge later. But for now, get it out of the way. I'll bet your kitchen already looks better.

Fill the bucket with water and put in some powdered detergent—not much, as just a bit goes a long way. Hot water is best; the hotter you can stand it, the better. Why? Because it will dry very fast and not leave streaks. Wet the microfiber cloth with the water in the bucket, and wring it out well.

Wipe down the upper cabinets by starting in a corner of the room and work your way around the room. Wipe down the handles or knobs. Next, clean the windows. When that is finished, wipe down all of the counters and then the lower cabinets, including the handles and knobs.

If your kitchen has a table and chairs, now is the time to get them cleaned. Fill the bucket with warm water and some of the powdered detergent. Wipe down the entire set. Table, chairs and if you have a fixture hanging above the table, clean it thorouly

Change the water in the bucket add some powdered detergent and wipe down the refrigerator, stove top and ovens. Pick up anything on the floor; then sweep or vacuum. Put a towel or knee pad under your knees to protect them while you wash the floor. Start at one end of the kitchen, and work your way out of the room. Wait for the floor to dry; then dump the water out.

Use the appropriate products to clean your stainless-steel appliances, stone counters, and wood or stone floors. Take the trash to its outside containers.

Put back the items on the fridge door. Return items to your countertops, but only those that are absolutely necessary. Learn to get along with less, and your kitchen will always appear clean.

Now let's talk about inside the fridge, ovens, and microwave and the stove-top burners. They all need to be kept clean and ready for action at any time, so don't forget to keep them on your cleaning schedule. Most ovens are self-cleaning these days, so read and follow the directions for cleaning them. The fridge is easy; keep a minimum number of items within it, and wipe the shelves, drawers, and doors often. The microwave is very easy. Fill a plastic bowl with water and the juice of one lemon; microwave on high for around five minutes; then take the bowl out, and wipe down inside. It will smell great, and the steam will help remove any food that is stuck to the walls.

If the grates over the burners are in bad shape, soak them overnight in hot water and some powdered detergent. The next morning put them in the dishwasher, and let them go through a cycle. That should do the trick, but if not, get a pot big enough to handle one piece at a time. Fill the pot with Coca Cola, and heat it up; bring it to a boil then soak the grate in it. Use a very stiff brush to scrub each piece. Of course, if they are so bad that they are unusable, then replace them. Call the manufacturer; go to the hardware store, or order online. Don't worry about replacing these items as they are inexpensive.

If the kitchen cabinets are bulging at the seams, go through them and get rid of some of the contents. There are charities waiting to put your items to good use. Everyone wins, and your kitchen cabinets will be organized to work for you rather than against you.

To clean the kitchen sink, wet a microfiber cloth, take a bar of soap, and rub the cloth with it, making it very sudsy. Wipe down the sink; then rinse and dry it. If your sink is stainless steel, it will almost look brand new. If you have a porcelain sink, wipe it down using powdered and liquid detergent. Scrub well, and then rinse and the sink should look almost new. Wipe down the faucet soap pump and the hot water tap as well. Dry and return everything to your bucket, and place it on the floor in the kitchen.

It is now time to vacuum the entire house, from one end to the other. The point of doing this last is so you won't walk over what you've already vacuumed. If you live in a two-story house, start upstairs at the farthest point from your stairway. Close the windows before you start to vacuum. Start on one side, and move across the room, side to side. If something needs to be moved, move it and return it exactly where it was. Work your way out of the room. When you are finished, there will be no footprints on the carpet. Move on to the next room and repeat the process, always making sure to go from side to side as you work your way out of the room, being careful not to leave any footprints. Work your way into the hallway and down the stairs.

If the house is all on one level, use the same process. Working your way out of every room, closing the windows and turning off the lights as you go. After you have finished the hallway and entryway, assuming there is carpet there, move on to the living room, dining room, and family room, working your way toward the front door. Once you've arrived there, it's over; you have cleaned your home. Everything has been put in order, and you can now live as you always have. This process will need to be repeated weekly or once every other week, if you can get away with it. If you are able to wait until every third or fourth week, that's okay too. Whatever works for your home is what is appropriate for you. Remember to keep it simple. You probably noticed that I changed out cleaning products many different times to clean the same surfaces. That was to let you know that there are many products for the same surfaces. Don't be afraid to try something new, it may work better for you.. Now on to the main event. The spring clean.

Spring Cleaning—
Bringing Home the Gold

Here comes the fun. Remember everything does not have to be accomplished in one day during spring cleaning. Take your time, and do one project a week or every other week—whatever works for you. None of this is written in stone. The plan can be changed often, if need be. Just remember, if you keep your house, it will keep you. Let's get started, and cross that bridge into the great unknown.

The First Steps
1. Forget about all of the regular cleaning, and concentrate on the parts of the house that need your attention once or twice during the year.
2. Each room will have something that needs to be done. Start by making a list of what needs to be done in each room. For the purposes

of this book, I'll use the home we "cleaned" together earlier.

Before you start, put together a folder that will hold the spring-cleaning schedule. If items in many rooms are bundled together, imagine the extension to your free time. Use the following lists as a model for your own.

The Spring Clean List

1. Send out all bedding and window treatments for cleaning. Many companies will pick up, deliver, and rehang your drapery.
2. Schedule time to have the furniture shampooed or dry-cleaned.
3. Schedule time to have the windows and screens washed.
4. Schedule time to have the walls washed.
5. Send out any Oriental carpets for cleaning
6. Schedule time to have the hardwood floors, tile, and stone floors cleaned and resealed.
7. Schedule time to have the carpeting cleaned and stretched if needed.

Work off this list, and add your own items to it. There are services for almost anything you want to have done these days, so talk to your friends and see which companies they've used. If you schedule everything properly, your home can be cleaned in about two weeks. It will take longer to get back carpets, drapery, and blinds, so send them out before you start cleaning the house.

The Bathroom

The List

1. Since this room is cleaned on a regular basis, there won't be much to do. . put the medicine cabinet on your list.
2. The vanity; take everything out and clean it thoroughly.
3. Linen closet; remove all items and wash down the inside.

The Clean

1. Remove all items from the medicine cabinet, one shelf at a time. Fill the sink with hot water; add some bleach, and a few drops of liquid detergent. Put on gloves if you want to, and remove the first shelf. Whether its glass or metal, put it in the sink. Wash it using a microfiber cloth; rinse it off, and dry. Then wet the cloth, wring it out, and wipe down the inside of the cabinet, the sides, the top, and the back. Return the shelf, and wipe down all of the items before returning them

to the cabinet. Get rid of unwanted items. Continue down to the next shelf, repeating the same steps until you have finished.

2. Clean the vanity drawers first. Remove all of the items from one drawer, and then wet the microfiber cloth using the hot-water mixture, wring it out, and use it to wipe the inside of the drawer. If necessary, use some baking soda on spots in the drawer. Then rinse out the drawer, and dry it completely. Return the items to each drawer after you've washed it, first removing those items you no longer need. Turn your attention to the center of the vanity. Remove all items, and wash down the entire inside, including the walls, base, and the insides of the doors. Next, organize this space. There are many containers available that can hold all of the items hiding here; one source is the Container Store (www. containerstore.com). You don't need to do everything at once; organizing piecemeal is fine. Look for ideas, and then find your own way of making them work.

3. Remove all items from the linen closet, one shelf at a time. Fill a bucket with a mixture of hot water, bleach, and liquid detergent. Start by wiping down the first shelf, i.e., the sides and the top. Return the items to the shelf, or

throw away items that are not worth saving. When you return towels to this space, fold and line them up neatly. Move on to the next shelf, and repeat this action until you have reached the bottom, then wash the floor and the door as well. Do not use the bleach on wooden doors; use a mixture of hot water and some powdered detergent. Finally, dry the doors after you are done.

The Master Bedroom

Concentrate on those items that really need your attention.

The List
1. Walls
2. Bedding and drapery
3. Floors, doors, and wood trim
4. Closet and side drawers

The Clean

After removing all art and photos use a brush to go over the ceilings and walls before beginning to clean.

1. Take one wall at a time; put some towels along the baseboards. Fill a bucket with warm water, and add some liquid detergent. Use a sponge and wash from bottom to top, one

section at a time. Dry the wall with a towel. To remove spots, put some baking soda on a microfiber cloth and rub. Rinse and dry. Continue by moving around the room until all of the walls have been scrubbed clean.

2. Send the bedding and drapes out to be cleaned at least once a year, including the bed skirts and all of the pillows. Down pillows should be washed have new stuffing and new ticking added to them. This is a good time to replace your bed padding; buy a new one. If the one you have is still in good shape, then get it cleaned with the bedding. Of course, you can also go to the Laundromat and clean everything on your own. If your drapes are pleated, remember to remove and rehang them properly. There are also companies that will remove and replace your blinds.

3. Remove all items from the floor. If you store items beneath the bed, remove them too. Take the bedding off the bed, and then the mattresses from the frame. Vacuum the frame of the bed, and the floor under the bed. If you have a headboard, wipe it down. Return your mattresses to the bed frame, and make the bed.

If your floors are wood, wash, reseal, and wax them, if appropriate. Whether your home has wood floors or carpet, consider hiring a professional once a year to clean them. If there are problems, this will be the time to solve them. Maybe your carpet needs to be stretched or maybe the wood needs to be screened and re-sealed Again, remember nothing was built in a day; take your time, do it the right way, and it will be there for you to enjoy forever.

Move onto the doors and the trim. Add some Bio Green Clean to a bucket of warm water; wet your microfiber cloth, and wipe down the doors, baseboards, crown molding, and door and window trimTo clean windows, remove the screens and take them outside. Fill a bucket with warm water, and add some detergent. Take a scrubbing brush, scrub the screens, and rinse them off with the hose. If taking them outside is not possible, then put them in the tub. Put a towel down on the bottom (to prevent scratching), and add the screens. Then use the same method described above; let them stand in the tub to dry. Washing the windows is not hard and takes no time at all. Fill a spray bottle with warm water, add five or six drops of liquid detergent, and spray the window. Use a brush, like a foxtail brush, to brush the window; then take a squeegee and wipe. Wipe the edges with a dry towel; then move onto the next window. Continue around the room until you have washed all the interior windows. Then go outside and repeat until all the windows are done. Before replacing the screens, remember to clean the tracks to the windows. You can use a brush for this and then wipe down afterwards, or you can vacuum the tracks then wipe down. Either way, remember to get the tracks clean. You can spray them with a silicon spray afterwards to make your windows move more freely. Replace the screens, and you're good to go. Once the blinds or draperies are clean and dry, rehang them

4. If you have chests of drawers, remove everything from one drawer. Fill a bucket with warm water, add some Bio Green Clean, and wipe out the drawer. Dry with a clean towel. Throw away items that you no longer need, and return the rest to the drawer. Fold clothes; you will be surprised how much more you can get into your drawer if everything is replaced neatly. Continue until all of the drawers have been cleaned.

5. Get your empty bag ready; it's time to remove items you no longer need from the closet.

Start at the top, and go systematically through each section. Look for anything you no longer use: clothing, belts, shoes, purses, and bags of all kinds as well as the boxes that contain those items. Put aside anything suitable for transport to a shelter, consignment store, church or other religious entity, or veterans' organization. This is the time to remember those who need help.

Fill a bucket with warm water, and add some Bio Green Clean; wet your microfiber cloth or sponge. Start at the top of the closet, and wipe down the shelves; then move onto the hanging sections, and then onto drawers, if you have them. Once you finish brushing and wiping, put things in order. Use containers that will hold your items neatly, such as those sold by the Container Store. Or get creative with your own containers, but put things in order. You can't wear what you can't see. Get one kind of hanger to keep everything uniform throughout. That goes for the containers too, even if you use shoe boxes. Make sure that everything is visible. Hang clothing properly. Hang ties and belts on a tie circle. Put shirts in see-through containers if you do not have the room to hang them. Try to keep the floor clear, although this is next to impossible. I don't think I've ever been in any closet in which the floor is perfectly clear.

6. You're almost there. Be sure to include pieces of furniture—chairs, ottomans, etc.—on the list of things to be cleaned. This includes slip covers, which can be sent to the cleaners with the bedding. They will come back clean and wrinkle free. If you have a steamer, then you might want to wash them yourself and steam out the wrinkles. If you do, make sure to wash them in cold water and Woo lite.

You are done. Wow; who knew that would be so easy? Put the room back together. Rehang the items on the walls, make the bed, and close the closet doors. The floors will be the very last item on the list; hire a professional to come in and clean them all, whether wood, carpet, tile, or cement.

The Teenager's Bedroom
When you tell your teenager that you're going in to his room to do a spring clean, he'll look at you like you've lost your mind. Let him know that as long as he helps, nothing that he wants to keep will find its way to the trash bin.

The List
1. Bedding and window treatments

2. Walls, floors, doors, and wood trim
3. Closets and side drawers
4. Furniture

The Clean

1. Send the bedding and window treatments out to be cleaned. Send any slip covers out as well. There are services that will clean and rehang blinds in one day. If your house is filled with blinds, schedule to have them cleaned at the same time.

2. Remove everything from the walls. Brush away the dust and cobwebs; this should include the ceiling too. Pull furniture away from the walls, and put towels along the baseboards. Fill a bucket with warm water, and add some liquid detergent—not too much, don't go crazy with the bubbles. Start from the bottom of the wall, and work your way up to the top. Work in sections as you go around the room.

   Dry the walls with a towel as you go. Wipe down the baseboards, crown molding, trim around the doors and windows, as well as the doors. Change the bucket water whenever it gets dirty. Remember all of the floors throughout the house will be done at the same time.

To clean windows, remove the screens and take them outside. Fill a bucket with warm water, and add some detergent. Take a scrubbing brush, scrub the screens, and rinse them off with the hose. If taking them outside is not possible, then put them in the tub. Put a towel down on the bottom (to prevent scratching), and add the screens. Then use the same method described above; let them stand in the tub to dry. Washing the windows is not hard and takes no time at all. Fill a spray bottle with warm water, add five or six drops of liquid detergent, and spray the window. Use a brush, like a foxtail brush, to brush the window; then take a squeegee and wipe. Wipe the edges with a dry towel; then move onto the next window. Continue around the room until you have washed all the interior windows. Then go outside and repeat until all the windows are done. Before replacing the screens, remember to clean the tracks to the windows. You can use a brush for this and then wipe down afterwards, or you can vacuum the tracks then wipe down. Either way, remember to get the tracks clean. You can spray them with a silicon spray afterwards to make your windows move more freely. Replace the screens, and you're good to go. Once the blinds or draperies are clean and dry, rehang them.

3. Change the water in the bucket, and add some Bio Green Clean. Wet a microfiber cloth, and dive into the closet. Put any items that are no longer worn or needed into bags. Go through the closet systematically, and try to remove as much as possible. Maybe you'll be lucky, and your teenager will let you throw away anything that you want to. Let him know that by helping others he is helping himself. Take a brush, and brush down the closet. Start at the top, and work your way down to the floor. Wipe down the closet from top to bottom; remove everything from the floor, and wipe it too. Then it is time to think about organizing.

My favorite store is the Container Store, but you can create your own system. Look around and get ideas, then adapt them to your own needs. You want your kid to be able to see what he has; keep that in mind when you are reorganizing. Adding all new hangers is a good idea; it gives the closet uniformity and makes it easier to find items. Get shoe boxes or shoe trees and hangers for belts, ties, and scarves. Add boxes for sweaters, hats, etc. Put things away, but make sure you can see them. Once the closet is finished, move onto the side drawers in the room. Change the water in the bucket, and add some Bio Green Clean. Remove all of the items from a drawer, and wash the inside. Use some baking soda, and scrub away any spots. Rinse and dry the drawer. Get rid of all items that are no longer being used. Fold anything that needs to be, and return those items to the drawer. Move onto the next drawer, and continue until you have cleaned them all.

4. If furniture pieces need to be cleaned, either wash them yourself or send them out with the bedding. If the pieces should be shampooed, schedule that for when you shampoo all of the furniture in the home.

The Baby's Room

In a baby's room, the first thought may be to disinfect everything in sight. Of course, that is the right approach. Get out the Lysol disinfectant, and begin.

The List

1. Bedding and window treatments
2. Walls, doors, floors, and trim
3. Closet and side drawers
4. Furniture

The Clean

1. Remove the bedding and window treatments, and send them to the cleaners. Alternatively, clean them yourself, if your washer is large enough, or take them to the Laundromat, and get everything done at the same time. Some Laundromats have drop-off services, which is worth the extra expense. Be flexible. If you want to clean the blinds yourself, do so. But wash the windows and screens before you start: {a} Vacuum the screen, window sill, and the trim around the window. (b) Using a spray bottle filled with warm water and a few drops of liquid detergent, spray the window. Then use a sponge to go over window, removing all of the spots. Get rid of the excess water with your squeegee, and wipe down the edges with a dry towel. Repeat this action with each window until you are done. To wash the blinds, fill a bucket with warm water, and add some Bio Green Clean. Wipe the blinds, starting at the top and working your way down to the bottom. Be sure to wipe both sides as you go. To save time, use a service that will sonically clean them for you.

2. Take everything off the walls; then use a brush to remove the dust and cobwebs off

the ceiling and walls. Place towels along the baseboards of one wall, and fill a bucket with warm water, and add a little liquid detergent. Starting at the bottom and working your way to the top, sponge off the walls. Do one section of the wall at a time, moving around until the entire room has been washed. Then wash the doors and trim, crown moldings, To clean windows, remove the screens and take them outside. Fill a bucket with warm water, and add some detergent. Take a scrubbing brush, scrub the screens, and rinse them off with the hose. If taking them outside is not possible, then put them in the tub. Put a towel down on the bottom (to prevent scratching), and add the screens. Then use the same method described above; let them stand in the tub to dry. Washing the windows is not hard and takes no time at all. Fill a spray bottle with warm water, add five or six drops of liquid detergent, and spray the window. Use a brush, like a foxtail brush, to brush the window; then take a squeegee and wipe. Wipe the edges with a dry towel; then move onto the next window. Continue around the room until you have washed all the interior windows. Then go outside and repeat until all the windows are done. Before replacing the screens, remember to clean the tracks to the windows. You can use a brush for this and then wipe down afterwards, or you can vacuum the tracks then wipe down. Either way, remember to get the tracks clean. You can spray them with a silicon spray afterwards to make your windows move more freely. Replace the screens, and you're good to go. Once the blinds or draperies are clean and dry, rehang them.

Baseboards, and wainscoting. If spots need to be removed, use some baking soda and scrub them clean. Rinse the area, and dry with a clean towel. Clean the floors last, using a professional, if possible.

3. put the closet in order, because you want to be able to find everything at a glance. You don't want to have to dig for something at the last moment only to find out that you no longer have any on hand. Take out everything from the closet; then take a brush and go over the entire interior, removing all of the dust and cobwebs. Fill a bucket with warm water, add some of the Lysol, and wipe down inside the closet, including the rods and the shelves. Wash the floor; then organize the space. Of course, my favorite store for this is the Container Store. Get ideas

and put them to use for yourself. Rehang everything, and add see-through boxes to the shelves so that you'll know what is there. Fold all of the items that need to be folded, and return them to the closet. Move onto the side drawers. Remove all of the items from one drawer and, after filling a bucket with warm water and adding some Lysol, wipe out the drawer, using baking soda for any spots. Rinse thoroughly, and dry with a towel. Remove all of those items that you no longer need and put them in a bag so you can take them to a charity of your choice. Fold items before returning them to the drawer, and move onto the next one. Keep everything neat so you know what you have and what you need to buy for the little one. Continue working around the room until all of the furniture has been washed, including the changing table. Make sure you use Lysol disinfectant to scrub this last item clean.

4. If you have a rocker with removable padding, wash it and let it air dry. If the chair has a slip cover, send it out to be cleaned with the bedding. Or wash it yourself, and send it to be pressed. Or steam it yourself, once it has been put back on the chair. Alternatively, schedule a time for all the furniture to be

cleaned by a professional. Sometimes toy boxes have a padded top for seating; this pad can be cleaned by vacuuming, then spraying with a cleaner like Bio Green Clean. Just spray and use a clean towel to wipe over the top until all spots have been removed. Bio Green Clean will take out all of the odors. Remember, it is a plant-based product and cannot harm your child.

The Living Room

When you are in the more formal side of the home, it's time to get even more fastidious about cleaning. In other words, look at every nook and cranny. Keeping a folder with suggestions for spring cleaning will help. Making it simple will be even more appreciated, because of the time you will save for yourself.

The List

1. Ceiling, walls, floors, trim, baseboards, and moldings
2. Drapery and blinds
3. Windows and screens
4. Furniture and artworks

The Clean

1. Remove everything from the walls; then brush the entire ceiling and all of the walls,

removing all of the cobwebs and dust. Be sure to clear the dust from any recessed lighting. Then wash the walls. To a bucket of warm water, add some liquid detergent; just a few drops will go a long way. Put towels on the floors along the baseboards; wet a sponge, wring it out; then take a section of wall at a time, and wash it from floor to ceiling. To clean spots, put some baking soda on a rag and rub clean; then rinse it with clean water and dry. Work your way around the room, one section at a time, until you have completed all the walls. As you go around the room, wipe down the trim, baseboards, moldings, and wainscoting. Change the water and detergent in your bucket as often as needed.

2. Scheduling is important here, so plan carefully and send out all drapery and blinds to be cleaned. Set this up before you clean the room so that they can be returned by the time you've finished. Of course, you can do all of this work yourself. Vacuum the drapery and the blinds; then remove the curtains, wash them at a Laundromat, have them pressed by a cleaner, and then rehang in the room.

3. Blinds can be washed in their place, whether they are Venetian, micro, mini, verticals, or plantation shutters. They can all be cleaned without too much trouble. Warm water and some liquid detergent are just fine for all of them. Waffle or fabric blinds also can be cleaned at home. Remove them from the windows, and fill up the tub with warm water and some liquid detergent but not too much. If the blinds are white, add about half a cup of bleach to the water. Mix it up well, add the blinds, and let them soak for about ten to fifteen minutes. Rinse them with clear water and hang them up to dry. Keep fabric verticals in place, and steam or you can shampoo them with fabric shampoo. Try a small section to see if it works well, and then clean each one. It should not take too long for them to dry. Don't be afraid to clean blinds yourself as it will save you an enormous sum of money. Sending everything out can be very expensive.

To clean windows, remove the screens and take them outside. Fill a bucket with warm 3.water, and add some detergent. Take a scrubbing brush, scrub the screens, and rinse them off with the hose. If taking them outside is not possible, then put them in the tub. Put a towel down on the bottom (to prevent scratching), and add the screens. Then use the same method described above; let them stand in the tub to dry. Washing the windows is not hard and takes no time at all. Fill a spray bottle with warm water, add five or six drops of liquid detergent, and spray the window. Use a brush, like a foxtail brush, to brush the window; then take a squeegee and wipe. Wipe the edges with a dry towel; then move onto the next window. Continue around the room until you have washed all the interior windows. Then go outside and repeat until all the windows are done. Before replacing the screens, remember to clean the tracks to the windows. You can use a brush for this and then wipe down afterwards, or you can vacuum the tracks then wipe down. Either way, remember to get the tracks clean. You can spray them with a silicon spray afterwards to make your windows move more freely. Replace the screens, and you're good to go. Once the blinds or draperies are clean and dry, rehang them.

4. Keeping to a schedule is very important. If you have your furniture professionally cleaned, put it on the schedule with the carpets, so that all can be finished at the same time. If

you decide to clean your own furniture, mix together a quarter cup of laundry detergent and one cup of warm water and blend together until it forms peaks that stay up by themselves. Vacuum the piece to be cleaned, and take the mixture and add it to a small piece of fabric with a brush. Work it into the fabric until the dirt mixes with the suds; then scrape them off, and wipe down with a clean cloth. If that does not work, then you might want to hire a professional to do the job;

This is also the time to wash your lamp shades. Remove them from the lamps. Fill the tub with warm water, add some liquid detergent, and mix well. Add one shade at a time to the tub. Fill a cup with the soapy water, and pour over the shade until it is thoroughly wet. Then use a soft rag to wash the shade, rinse with clear water, and put it on towels to dry. If your shades are white, add a little bleach to the water.

It's also important to clean your works of art, including oils, tapestries, statues, and even marble columns. If you are unsure how to handle any of these items, seek help from the professionals. I can't tell you how many times I've called the Art Institute of Chicago for advice about cleaning a piece.

It's important to get this right. To avoid devaluing your artworks, seek the help. This is one of those rare times when I leave it to the professionals. As preservationists, it's what they do best.

Finally, remove drawers from any cabinets in the room, and clean them out.

The Dining Room

Although this room is cleaned weekly, there will be pieces that need a good spring clean.

The List

1. Walls, crown moldings, chair rails, wainscoting, baseboards, window and door trim
2. Furniture, lighting, windows, draperies
3. Floors or carpets

The Clean

1. Remember the number-one rule: turn on the lights. Move furniture away from the walls, if necessary. Remove dust and cobwebs from the walls and ceiling with a brush. Fill a bucket with warm water and some liquid detergent. Place some towels along the baseboards, and start washing a section of wall, from bottom to top. Work your way around the room,

until all of the walls have been cleaned. Wash the baseboards, wainscoting, and trim as you go. Use baking soda and a microfiber cloth to clean any spots on the walls; then rinse thoroughly and dry.

2. Wash draperies, and then send them out to be pressed and rehung. Remove soft blinds and place them in a tub of warm water with some liquid detergent. If they are white, add some bleach to the water. Take a cup and pour the water from the tub over the blinds. Use a soft towel to scrub them clean, rinse with clear water, and hang to dry. If you have verticals, leave them in place, and use a fabric cleaner. A steamer will work just fine on these, removing spots and odors. You can, of course, send window treatments out to be cleaned. Check for specials in your area, and use them when you can. It will save a lot of time and money. To clean windows, remove the screens and take them outside. Fill a bucket with warm 3.water, and add some detergent. Take a scrubbing brush, scrub the screens, and rinse them off with the hose. If taking them outside is not possible, then put them in the tub. Put a towel down on the bottom (to prevent scratching), and add the screens. Then use the same method

described above; let them stand in the tub to dry. Washing the windows is not hard and takes no time at all. Fill a spray bottle with warm water, add five or six drops of liquid detergent, and spray the window. Use a brush, like a foxtail brush, to brush the window; then take a squeegee and wipe. Wipe the edges with a dry towel; then move onto the next window. Continue around the room until you have washed all the interior windows. Then go outside and repeat until all the windows are done. Before replacing the screens, remember to clean the tracks to the windows. You can use a brush for this and then wipe down afterwards, or you can vacuum the tracks then wipe down. Either way, remember to get the tracks clean. You can spray them with a silicon spray afterwards to make your windows move more freely. Replace the screens, and you're good to go. Once the blinds or draperies are clean and dry, rehang them

Have the chair cushions professionally cleaned, or clean them yourself. First, vacuum the entire chair, removing crumbs from any pleats. Remove spots with a professional spot remover. Spray on the spot, let it stand for a few minutes, use a wet towel to rub the spot clean, and let it dry before continuing. Then mix a tablespoon of laundry detergent in a bucket of warm water, get it lathered up, and apply it to your chairs with a soft brush. Using a wet towel, remove any excess liquid from each chair and let it dry overnight. Move onto the drawers and cabinets in the room. Remove all of the items, and clean out the insides. Add some Bio Green Clean to a bucket of warm water, and use it to wash the insides of each drawer and cabinet. Use baking soda on the spots. Then wipe down all of the items you removed, and return them to the drawers and cabinets.

Clean all the lights in the room, from recessed lighting and chandeliers to sideboard lamps and wall sconces. Since lighting sets the mood, it's very important to get this right in the dining room. Make sure to clean each piece thoroughly. Wipe down brass or silver linings with warm water and vinegar. Use the vinegar and warm water to clean glass or crystal sconces or chandeliers. If the sconces are metal, then find the appropriate cleaner and let it work its magic. Don't forget to clean the lampshades and candlesticks. If you have a crystal candelabra or crystal candlesticks, use vinegar and warm water and dry when done. If they are made of a metal like brass or silver, then clean them with an appropriate product.

3. Take care of wood floors and carpets at the end of the spring cleaning; hire a professional to clean them all at one time. If there is an Oriental carpet in this room, then send it out for cleaning well before you finish cleaning the room. You can also turn your carpet over, and vacuum it, using the beater brushes to remove as much dirt as possible. This is something that you should do on your own once in a while anyway, but washing carpets requires drying racks, which most homes do not have. You don't have to send them out every year; once every five to seven years is a good space of time. If you do it more often, the threads will break down much faster. Get them repaired, if necessary, while they are being cleaned. Conserving your carpets will give you many years of use.

The Family Room

One of the most used rooms in the home today, the family room will need lots of attention. If you send out window treatments, and carpets for cleaning, schedule them to be returned on the day you complete the room cleaning.

The List

1. Walls, trim, moldings, wainscoting
2. Window treatments and windows
3. Furniture and floors

The Clean

1. Jump right into the thick of it, and remove everything from the walls, including art and photographs. Move any furniture that can be moved away from the walls. Brush the ceiling and walls, removing any dust and cobwebs. If you have recessed lighting with a brass or chrome lining, wipe with a little vinegar and water mixture, and then dry. Place towels along the baseboards of one wall, and fill a bucket with warm water and some liquid detergent. Don't go crazy with the detergent; just a few drops will do. Wash a section of the wall, from bottom to top, using a large sponge. Remove spots with a microfiber cloth and some baking soda; then rinse and dry. Wash the baseboards, crown molding, wainscoting, trim and door jambs as you go. Change the water as needed, and move onto the next section of the wall, working your way around the room.

2. Send window treatments out for cleaning, or consider cleaning them yourself. Remove

drapes, take them to a Laundromat, and wash them; then take them to cleaners to press and rehang for you. Place soft blinds in a tub filled with warm water and a little liquid soap. If the blinds are white, add a little bleach to the water. Rinse them with clear water, and hang them to dry. Leave plantation shutters and metal blinds in place and wash them one slat at a time, from top to bottom, using some warm water and a little bleach. Work your way from side to side. There are also companies that will take metal blinds off your windows and put them in an ultrasound bath, returning them the same day. If you have fabric verticals, you can use a fabric spray cleaner and a steamer, if you have one. Try a small spot first to make sure that the cleaner will do what you want it to; if not send the blinds out for cleaning, or hire a company to clean them on site. Send swags and tails out or vacuum them; then use a steamer to go over each one. Remember steam and water can shrink material, so be very careful and take your time. Try a small section of material and see what happens. If there is shrinkage, stop, and have them professionally cleaned. . To clean windows, remove the screens and take them outside.

Fill a bucket with warm 3.water, and add some detergent. Take a scrubbing brush, scrub the screens, and rinse them off with the hose. If taking them outside is not possible, then put them in the tub. Put a towel down on the bottom (to prevent scratching), and add the screens. Then use the same method described above; let them stand in the tub to dry. Washing the windows is not hard and takes no time at all. Fill a spray bottle with warm water, add five or six drops of liquid detergent, and spray the window. Use a brush, like a foxtail brush, to brush the window; then take a squeegee and wipe. Wipe the edges with a dry towel; then move onto the next window. Continue around the room until you have washed all the interior windows. Then go outside and repeat until all the windows are done. Before replacing the screens, remember to clean the tracks to the windows. You can use a brush for this and then wipe down afterwards, or you can vacuum the tracks then wipe down. Either way, remember to get the tracks clean. You can spray them with a silicon spray afterwards to make your windows move more freely. Replace the screens, and you're good to go.

Once the blinds or draperies are clean and dry, rehang them

3. Empty the wall units, and get ready to wash them down from top to bottom. Fill a bucket with warm water, and add some Bio Green Clean. If your unit has an exposed top, then vacuum it before you wipe it down. Move onto the inside of the unit, and wipe down all of the shelves and drawers. Remove spots with some baking soda on a microfiber cloth. Rinse with clean water, and then dry. Wipe down all of the outside surfaces, and make sure they are streak free. Many wall units have outside surfaces made of many different materials. I've had to clean wood, laminate, , all types of metal, including stainless steel and steel, stone, and mirrors. Whatever the surface happens to be, use the right cleaner. If you are unsure what to use, call the manufacturer of the piece and ask for recommendations. Never be afraid to ask the professionals.

Put everything that belongs there back into the unit. Throw out what you no longer need, and clean all the pieces before you return them. Remove and clean the lampshades. Fill the tub with warm water and add some detergent. If your shades are white, add some bleach to the water. Rinse; then stand on towels to dry. Remove everything from the drawers of side tables, and wipe them out. Return the items to the drawers when done, first throwing away what you no longer use. Clean stand-alone art pieces. Again, call for help, if you need it; you do not want to devalue any of your art.

If your room is filled with plant life and trees, clean them as well. If you can, take them outside and use your hose to rinse them off. Add any soil that may be needed, give them a shot of food, let them dry, and return them to your room. Of course, you can clean the furniture, but you may want to turn it over to a professional because of the heavy use this room gets. If you are up to it, start by vacuuming the pieces. Then mix together a quarter cup of laundry detergent and one cup of warm water; blend together until you get stiff peaks just like whipped cream. Using a brush, take some of the mixture, place it on the fabric, and work it into the material until the dirt comes out in the mixture. Remove with a clean towel, and move onto the next section, until you have finished the whole piece. This is now the time to call in the professional for your piano. Have the interior cleaned and retuned. If parts need to be replaced get that done now. Your family room should be shining by now, so enjoy it until it's time to do it all over again.

The Laundry Room

This room can be tricky. It's usually filled with all those things we do not want in the rest of the house: coats, shoes, boots, cleaning supplies, laundry detergents, bleach, spot removers, clothes hanging up to dry, laundry baskets, and the proverbial trashcan. If you have cabinets above the laundry machines, chances are they are filled with supplies, paper goods, and possibly small tools.

The List
1. Remove all products from the room.
2. Walls, baseboards, trim, and doors
3. Washer, dryer, hot-water tank, and heating and air-conditioning units

The Clean
1. Remove everything that can be moved from the room, including items in the cabinets, anything hanging about, and articles on the floor. Disconnect the washer and dryer, and move them away from the wall. It's time to clean underneath and behind them.

Using the brush attachment, vacuum all of the dust from the backs of the machines, including the floor and walls. Then fill the bucket with warm water and some of the Bio Green Clean; use a microfiber cloth to wash the washer and dryer on all sides, including all of the attached hoses. For a very small fee, you can have the dryer hose cleaned professionally. I recommend doing this. Plugged hoses can cause fires and you don't want to risk the chance of that happening. Leave the machines where they are until you have washed the walls and trim.

2. Brush away all of the dust and the cobwebs from the walls and ceiling. Fill a bucket with warm water, and add a few drops of liquid detergent. Place towels at the baseboards, and wash the wall from bottom to top. Remove spots with some baking soda; then rinse with clear water and dry. Work your way around the room; then move onto the trim and baseboards. If this room has a window, remove and wash the screen. If you have a window in this room, 1. Remove the screens and wash them with soapy water, then rinse and let them dry. 2. Fill a bottle with warm water and a few drops of liquid detergent. 3. Spray window and using your

sponge go over window to remove any dirt. 4. Use your squeegee to remove the water from the window, and then take a dry towel and go around the edges. 5. Wash out the tracks to the window, then return the screens before returning the washer and dryer to the wall, wash the floor. Fill a bucket with warm water and some of the Bio Green Clean. Take a brush and go over the floor where the machines will go; then using a microfiber cloth to wipe up the water from the floor. Then put the machines back into place. First, attach the washer hoses to their faucets; then reattach the dryer hose to its connection and move the machines back into their rightful places. You may have to rebalance the machines by adjusting the legs on each piece. Plug them back in, and you're ready to go again.

3. This room may house the hot-water tank and heating and air-conditioning units. Take a brush and go over these pieces of equipment. You can wipe them down, but be careful; they have wires and switches that should not be moved. For example, you do not want to change the temperature of the hot-water tank and burn or freeze someone taking a shower. However, this is a good time to change the

filter in the heating and air-conditioning unit. Next move on to the cabinets in the room. Fill a bucket with warm water, add some Bio Green Clean, and wipe out the cabinets, including the sides, tops, and bottoms of shelves and the doors, inside and out. Remove spots with some baking soda and a microfiber cloth. Wipe until gone, rinse with clear water, and then dry. Return all of the items to the cabinets, getting rid of anything you no longer need. For toxic products, call a waste-removal company to find out how to handle; search online for companies in your area.

Finish the cabinets by washing all of the products that will be returned to the shelves. Put back the shoes, boots, and the trash can. Remember the floors will be done at the end of our clean.

The Entryway

Of course, this is a very important room. Keeping it clean and in order is of great importance. It is the first impression that someone gets of you and your home, so make it sparkle.

The List

1. Walls, moldings, trim, and doors

2. Lighting and windows
3. Furniture, coat closet, and floors

The Clean

1. First, turn on the lights. Remove everything from the walls, and pull the furniture away too. Take your brush, and remove dust and cobwebs from the walls and ceiling. Place towels along the baseboards to catch any dripping as you wash the walls. Fill a bucket with warm water, and add a few drops of liquid detergent. Then wash the wall from bottom to top. If there is wainscoting, baseboards, or crown molding in the entryway, wipe each section as you go. Remove spots with some baking soda and your microfiber cloth; rinse with clear water, and dry with a clean towel. Move around the entryway until you have washed all of the walls. Also wash down the front door and closet doors if you have them. Refill your bucket with warm water, add some liquid detergent, wet your microfiber cloth, and use it to wipe down the doors. Be sure to get the trim as well. If your front door is made of something other than wood—for example, stainless steel, glass, or rare wood—use the appropriate cleaner. Look in the products list to find the right cleaner for your door.

2. Your windows need to shine; take your time to wash and dry them. If you have a two- or three-story entryway, call a professional, unless you enjoy climbing and have the proper equipment to do this safely. You may have a grand chandelier that needs to be lowered to be cleaned, a lantern, or recessed lighting. Whatever type of lighting you have, make it shine when you are finished. Use vinegar and water for all of the glass pieces. You may have sconces on the walls; if so polish the brass or silver parts, and wash the glass with vinegar and warm water; then dry. If you have shades, wash them with some warm water and liquid detergent. Dip them into the mixture, and rinse them clean with clear water. Then put on a towel to dry.

3. Return furniture pieces to their appropriate places. Clean any mirrors at this point. Window cleaner will work just fine here. Then clean the furniture pieces. If they are wood, you may want to add some wax. Once or twice a year is a good schedule for adding wax to any furniture. Go to the products list to find the right type of wax.

   Remove all of the items from furniture the drawers, particularly all of those items you no longer need or use. Put them in the charity pile. Wash the inside of the drawers. Fill a bucket with some warm water and some laundry detergent. Remove spots using some baking soda and a microfiber cloth; rinse and dry. Return all the items to the drawers, and move onto the closet.

Organize the closet to ensure the best use of the space. Remove everything, including all of the coats, shoes, etc. Take your brush, and remove dust and cobwebs from the walls and ceiling. Fill a bucket with warm water and liquid detergent, and add some towels along the baseboards of the closet to catch any drips. Wash the ceiling with a sponge, and then the walls, one section at a time, again moving from bottom to top. Use some baking soda and a microfiber cloth and remove any spots. Rinse with clear water; then dry with a towel. Then put everything back. Remember to organize. Add clear boxes for gloves, scarves, and hats. If you need shoe bins, then get them; they will save space. Sometimes just a rug under the shoes is enough to catch the dust and dirt. The rug can always be put into the washer for cleaning. One more little trick here is to get the same type of hangers for all the coats. Not only will the coats look good, they also will hang properly and will not need to be cleaned as often. Part with anything that you can to free up space and also help someone in need. Many cities organize coat drives for the needy; think about donating to one of those services. Call your local city hall to get the details.

If your entryway has an Oriental or designer carpet, send it out for cleaning with the rest of the carpets, so that they can all return at the same time.

Well, this brings us to the last room, the kitchen. You may ask, why did we wait so long to get to this room? Many may be glad it took so long to get here, but for me it is purely standard practice. We needed the sink for water to clean the other rooms. But this next room is going to take some time, so be prepared. Take a break, have some coffee or a stiff drink, maybe a nap—whatever works. Either way we are heading into the abyss, so buck up and get ready to organize the hardest room in your home.

The Kitchen

If this were a couple hundred years ago, cleaning the kitchen might have been as easy as throwing a bucket of water onto the floor and sweeping it out the door. Aren't you lucky you live in modern times?

Technology has taken cleaning this room to new heights of grandeur. Pay attention because so much happens in this room. The kitchen is where we eat, snack, party, talk about our problems, and solve our financial woes. We celebrate life on many levels there, from feeding the baby to making tea for our grandparents. Let's get started. Turn on the lights, and take a good look at the room. Remove all of the chairs. Then take everything off the counters and put it on the kitchen table. Remove everything from the walls and also anything that does not belong on the floor.

The List
1. Walls, ceilings, moldings, trim, baseboards, lighting
2. Cabinets and windows
3. Appliances and counters
4. Furniture and floors

The Clean
1. Using your brush, remove dust and cobwebs from the ceiling and walls. Fill a bucket with warm water, and add some Bio Green Clean. Look at the label to find the right amount of cleaner for the job at hand. Since this room is likely to have cooking oil stuck on the walls, you will need products of the proper strength to remove it. Bio Green

Clean is plant based and cannot hurt you, but the little munchkins within it will eat right through just about any type of dirt on your walls and ceiling. Place towels along the baseboards, and wash a section of wall at a time, from bottom to top. Move around the room until you have washed all the walls. Change the water, add more Bio Green Clean, and clean all of the moldings, baseboards, and trim. Use baking soda on a microfiber cloth to clean any spots; then use clear water to rinse and dry with a towel.

Because the cooking oil attaches itself to everything, you must wash the kitchen ceiling. Brushing should be enough for the ceilings in all of the other rooms. Take a sponge and, a section at a time, go across the whole room. When you are done, take a good look to see if you have left streaks. If you have, use clear water and go over those spots, then dry them with a towel. This should remove any streaks that may be left. Take this opportunity to wipe the recessed lighting, if you have any in the room. If you have a fluorescent light, remove the cover and wash it. Remove cobwebs in the light fixture with a dry towel. Clean the cover with some of the Bio Green Clean. Spray some on the inside of the fixture, and wipe it clean of all dust and bugs. Dry with a towel when done; then turn over, spray the top, and dry as before. Place the cover back onto fixture, and move onto any other hanging fixtures—pendants or a chandelier—in the room. Next, turn your attention to the backsplash, if you have one. Figure out what it is made of—mirrors, tile, copper, stainless steel, or glass—and what product you will need to clean it. Take your time, and do your homework.

2. The easiest way to clean a cabinet is to remove all of the items within it. Put some towels down on the counters, and place the items on top of them to avoid scratching the counters while cleaning the cabinets. Fill the bucket with warm water, and add some Bio Green Clean. If your shelves are removable, then remove them and place to the side. Take your microfiber cloth, and start wiping down the interior of the cabinet—the top, sides, and bottom. Don't forget to wipe the insides of the doors as well. Put some baking soda on a microfiber cloth to remove spots; then rinse and dry with a clean, dry towel. Use the same process to clean the shelves; then return them to their places in

the cabinet. If you use shelf paper, replace it at this time.

Return the items you took out of the cabinets. Remember to purge all of those items you no longer need; send them to organizations that can use them to help others. Don't forget to organize as you return your items. Go to the Container Store to find baskets and see-through boxes that will make it easier to see what you have. Fill the sink with warm water, add some liquid detergent, and wash all of the items before you return them. Dry them, and place them back into the cabinet. Arrange your shelves so you get the best use of the space. Make it easy to see what you have and to remove those items. If you have to pull things out to get to something else, you probably haven't placed it in the right cabinet. Think about how you use your kitchen, then put items back into those spaces that will make it easy to get to them. You always want to know what you have and what you need to get; that's why you want to keep the kitchen in order. No one has extra dollars these days to spend on items that are not needed.

Close the cabinet doors, and wipe down the outsides, knobs, or handles. Work around the room until all of the top cabinets are clean. Remember to think about what you can get rid of and how you can better use the cabinet. Don't be afraid to rearrange the cabinets and the rest of the kitchen so that it works for you in a more efficient way. When all the top cabinets are done, move onto the lower ones. Change the water, and add more Bio Green Clean to the bucket. Once again put the towels on the countertop, and place all of the items from each drawer onto the towels. Use a microfiber cloth to wipe down the drawer; then remove any spots with baking soda, rinse, and dry. Think about how the drawer can be organized to make it easier to use. Whether they are silverware, plastic utensils, or papers, look for the right containers in which to place them. Once everything has been washed, return the items to the drawer, except for those that will go to charity. Work your way around the room, until you have finished all of the cabinets.

Let's talk about materials that may need to be disposed of, those items under the sink that may be toxic. Look for disposal units in your area, or call your local city hall and ask for information about companies that do this work. If you need poisonous cleaners to clean your home, find the right containers to put them into and keep them away from children.

Today, there are containers for everything. If you are looking for a way to store your spices, there are steppers for drawers to hold them. If you have a pantry in your kitchen, this is a good place to use containers to store food of all types, from packets of soy sauce to cereal to olive oil to flour. Make this space really work for you. While you're in there, get rid of all of those items you no longer need. Food pantries and organizations for battered women will take many of your items. They may even pick them up; just call and ask. If your kitchen has other cubbies, then clean them as well. You may have a small appliance garage on your counter-top, or you may be real lucky and have a butler's pantry. Whatever the case may be, clean it, purge it of items you no longer need, and organize it to work for you more efficiently.

Make sure everything has been returned to its rightful place and that all of those items going to charity have been removed from the kitchen. Then move onto the windows. If you have window coverings, remove them, if you can. Send draperies out to be cleaned and pressed, or do them yourself. Wash them at a Laundromat; then take them to dry cleaners to be pressed. Blinds can be removed and washed. If they are soft blinds, fill the tub halfway with warm water and some liquid detergent—not too much, of course, or you'll overflow with bubbles. If your blinds are white, add half a cup of bleach to the water. Let the blinds soak in the water for about fifteen to twenty minutes; then let the water out of the tub, rinse the blinds with clear water, and hang to dry. If you have micro or mini blinds or verticals, send them to a company that will use ultrasound to clean them. Many of these services work onsite, and will finish in a day or less. Fabric verticals can be steam-cleaned. If you have your own steam cleaner, you can do this yourself. Just be careful. Try a spot to see if it dries well, and stop if it shrinks or alters the color. Once the blinds are out of the way, turn your attention to cleaning the windows.

Remove the screens, wash them with warm, soapy water; then rinse and let them air dry while you clean the windows. Fill a spray bottle with warm water, and add a few drops of liquid detergent. Spray the inside of the window; then take your sponge and remove all of the dust and any spots on the glass. Remove excess liquid with your squeegee, and dry the edges with a clean dry towel. Move onto the rest of the windows, repeating this process until you have finished. When you are done, repeat the same process with the outsides of the windows. Before Replacing the screens be sure to clean the tracks to the windows. Use a brush or vacuum them, but get them clean. you may want to add some silicon spray to them to make the window slide easier once the screens have been replaced, return your blinds and or draperies to the windows.

3. Appliances large and small, from the toaster to the refrigerator, all need a good cleaning. Start with your small appliances: toaster; the toaster oven; the mixers, both handheld and upright; juicers; blenders, etc. Fill the sink with warm water, add some Bio Green Clean, and use a microfiber cloth to wipe down these appliances. Then, return them to their rightful places. Here's a good hint: keep them off the counter and behind closed

doors. No one wants to see them, and they only take up space.

Next, move onto the largest appliances: refrigerator, ovens, dishwasher, microwave, including the vent over the stove top. There are companies that will clean these appliances. Depending on how dirty they are, you may want someone else to clean your ovens. Whether you have one oven or a double one, however, you can do this yourself. Most ovens today are self-cleaning and are not much trouble to clean. Read the directions in the owner's manual, and follow them exactly. Many older ovens are not self-cleaning, but can be cleaned by placing the racks and the bottom plate on newspapers, spraying them with Easy-Off, and letting them stay for a while, sometimes overnight. Spray the inside of the oven; this means the top, sides, and bottom (if you cannot remove the bottom plate). Let stand according to the directions; then wipe down, rinse, and dry. If the oven has hardened grease attached to it, take a razor-blade scraper and scrape it clean. Do this on the glass on the inside of the door as well; just be careful not to scratch the glass. You can minimize the chance of this happening by wetting the glass before you scrape. (This is also a good hint for cleaning windows; wet them before you scrape them.) The blade will work better if it is totally wet. Once the inside is clean, turn your attention to the racks. Take them, one at a time, to the sink, and remove the Easy-Off with warm water. I have found that the best way to do this is to run the water constantly, and use an S.O.S. or Billow pad. Or you can use a zero grade steel wool. This also will help to remove any burnt on grease. Do one side at a time, and then wipe with a towel to dry. Return the racks to the oven and close the doors. Use a microfiber cloth and some warm, soapy water to wash down the outsides of the oven doors; dry with a towel when done. Be careful with the digital equipment, or you could accidentally start the oven or reset the clock or timer.

If your stove top and oven is a single appliance, remove the drip pans. Spray them with Easy-Off, if you need to; otherwise, just put them into a bucket of hot water, and let them soak for a bit. Lift up the top of the stove and place the holding bar in its spot. Then take some hot water and some Bio Green Clean, and wash out underneath the top. Rinse and dry when done. Place the holding bar in its space, lower the top, and snap it back into place. Remove each drip pan, wash it with Bio Green Clean, and rinse when done. To get rid of burned-on grease and food, take the finest grade of steel-wool and rub over those spots. If your drip pans are beyond cleaning, make a trip to the store to purchase new ones. A set of four will cost around $30, but you may only need to replace one or two. Measure them, because they come in different sizes; you don't want to get home and find that you've purchased the wrong ones. Return them to the top of the stove after washing the top thoroughly. If you're top are a traditional one with a glazed top, use boiling water and a few drops of liquid detergent to clean grease or built-up food particles. Do not use anything that is abrasive or you may scratch the top and need to have it refinished. Boiling water can remove everything with a little bit of time. If your top is made of glass, there are nonabrasive cleansers that will remove just about everything. Find one that you like.

The best way to clean stainless steel is to use hot water and some liquid detergent.

Wet a small towel, add some of the detergent, and go over the stove top. Rinse with clear hot water; then dry with a towel. When I worked in restaurants, I used powdered detergent mixed with soda water, which made the stainless steel shine like a mirror, Make sure to use hot water, and then rinse and dry. Of course, the manufacturer's manual will tell you exactly how to clean your particular piece of equipment.

Move onto the hood above the stove top. First, remove the filter. I have cleaned filters in several ways throughout my career. One is to put it into the dishwasher. Another is to soak it in hot water and some powdered detergent; then rinse and let it dry. You also can spray it with Easy-Off; let it stand for a while; then rinse and air dry. Once the filter has been dealt with, turn to the hood itself. If it is in really bad shape, then spray it with Easy-Off, and let it stand for a while; remember you cannot spray any part of the hood that has been painted. The easy-off will eat right through the paint. Then remove the grease and dirt with a towel soaked in the hot water and powdered detergent. Rinse till clean, and then replace the filter. Move onto the light.

There will be a panel that can be removed; soak it in hot water with some powdered detergent. Remove the light bulb and wipe it clean; then replace it and the cover, after you've washed it. You might find that the lighting seems much brighter. Next, turn your attention to the outside of the hood. Use hot water and liquid detergent to wash down the outside; then rinse and dry. Hoods are made from many different types of materials, including copper, polished steel, and glass; find and use the cleaners that are appropriate for yours.

If you can, pull the refrigerator away from the wall. You won't need to clean the inside, because you do this on a regular basis, but pull it away from the wall so you can clean the entire outside. Take a brush, and clean the walls surrounding the refrigerator. Unplug the refrigerator for the time being so you can pull it further away, if necessary. Then vacuum the floor, baseboards, the back of the refrigerator, and the bottom rack at the base of the door. Fill a bucket with warm water, and add a few drops of liquid detergent. Place towels along the baseboards, and wash the walls from bottom to top. Then move onto the refrigerator itself. Change the water, and add more liquid detergent. Really wet the rag, add a few drops of the detergent, and place the rag on the top of the refrigerator. Go over the top and sides of the refrigerator. Stay away from the back if you have a cardboard cover; otherwise go over the back just as you did the top and sides. Rinse the rag, and go over the refrigerator again until you have removed all of the soap. Take a clean, dry towel, and go over the outside once more to dry and take all of the marks off the finish. Fill a bucket with clean water, add some liquid detergent, and go over the floor under the refrigerator. Use some baking soda to remove spots; then rinse and dry the floor.

Return the refrigerator to its location. Some people will not be able to move your refrigerators, because they are built into the kitchen cabinets. Still, the outsides still need to be attended to; make sure that they have been washed and dried. Maybe your fridge has wood panels that need to be waxed or stainless-steel panels that need to have a new coat of sealer. Whatever the case, get it done now and it will make it much easier to work going forward.

Move onto the microwave. Many are located above the stove top and are very easy to keep clean. Some are built into the cabinet. If this is the case, remove the oven, and wash the cabinet. Return the microwave, and plug it in. Fill a bucket with warm water and some of the liquid detergent; then wash the outside of the microwave. Use baking soda to remove spots; then rinse and dry.

Today many homes have built-in wine coolers; if you're one of the lucky ones, then this piece of equipment also needs to be cleaned. Wipe it down with warm water and some liquid detergent; then rinse and dry before adding your bottles. Make sure the outside of the dishwasher has been cleaned thoroughly. Use a microfiber cloth, some warm water, and liquid detergent, and wash the outside. Then rinse, and wipe down with a clean, dry towel. Do the same with the trash compactor, but this time use Bio Green Clean and go over the inside as well. If bits and pieces are attached to the container, get it very wet with Bio Green

Clean. Let it sit for about fifteen minutes; then rinse and dry.

Wow! All of the major and minor pieces of equipment have been cleaned as have the cabinets, walls, ceiling, windows, and window treatments. Let's move onto the countertops. By now, you know what I'm going to say. Remove everything from the counters. Fill the bucket with warm water, and add some liquid detergent. Use a microfiber cloth to cover the entire top with the mixture; get it very sudsy and work it into the top. You will be able to feel the top through the cloth. Keep cleaning until the top is smooth. Then rinse it off, and dry it with a clean dry towel. Believe me when I tell you this is the best method. Keep it simple, as they say. The goal is to remove all of the grease and grime from the countertops, so make this easy on yourself Liquid detergent is made for this kind of job. It will return your counters almost to their original state. Now is also the time to reseal stone countertops, which should happen at least once a year. This applies to the backsplash as well. Wash it, and reseal if it is made of stone.

4. If you are lucky enough to have room for a table and chairs in your kitchen, clean them as well. Remove all items from the tabletop, and put them back where they belong. Keep the top of the counters as clear as possible as you'll need to rest items there while you are working. Add items you no longer need to the box or bag going to charity. Fill a bucket with warm water, add some Bio Green Clean, wet a microfiber cloth, and wipe down the chairs. If they have removable seats, take them off. If necessary, send them out for cleaning with the draperies or blinds, so that they all return at the same time. If they are machine washable, put them in the washing machine with some Bio Green Clean, about a cup per load. Watch how clean and odor free they become. If the seat covers are permanently attached, put some Bio Green Clean in a bucket of warm water, and use a soft brush to go over the seat cover until all of the dirt is gone. Dry with a clean towel. Next, wipe down the table, using the same method applied to the counters. Whether the table is glass, chrome, high-end wood, or stone, scrub it free of all food or oil particles.

Remember that you will do all of the floors in the home at the same time, so now is the time to call in the professionals. Set time aside, and plan exactly what you want to have done. If you have sent out Oriental carpets, have them returned after your hard floors have been cleaned. Here is my usual plan for getting floors and other items cleaned by a professional:

1. Clean all the carpets. And have stretched where needed.
2. Clean the hardwood floors.
3. Clean tile and stone floors.
4. Steam- or dry-clean the furniture.
5. Return all Oriental carpets and throw rugs to their rightful places.
6. Have all blinds returned as well as all draperies replaced.

Figure out how long it will take for the rugs, blinds, and the draperies to be cleaned. Then schedule the cleaning of the floors accordingly. Of course, you'll have to be flexible; unexpected changes will occur. But, if you have done your homework, this process will run very smoothly. Although it's been a long race, you've made it across the finish line in first place. Congratulations! Your gold medal awaits.

There you have it. I've shown you how to clean your home on a weekly basis and also how to spring clean. Of course, there will be variations to everything I've set forth here. Changes will occur constantly. Your furnishings will change as will the products for cleaning them. Be very vigilant when choosing cleaning products. Stay away from chemicals that will harm you or anyone else. Finally, remember to keep it clean and, above all, to keep it simple.

The End

Index

E

Easy-Off spray, 23–24, 136, 139
Enamel, 18
Entryway
        cleaning process, 77–78
        spring cleaning, 123–127

F

Family room
        cleaning process, 67–70
        spring cleaning, 114–120
Feather duster, 69
Floors, 114, 145
Formica, 18–19
Fruit fly, 19
Furniture
        kitchen, 144
        moving, 115
        spring cleaning, 125–126

G

Gelcoat, 19
Goddards, 29
Gold, 19
Granite, 19–20
Grease, 20

H

Harrell's, 34
Heating units, 122–123
Hot-water-tank, 122–123
House rhythm, 57

I

Ivory liquid soap, 13–14, 20, 28

J

Johnson's paste wax, 14

K

Kitchen
        cabinets, 130–133
        cleaning process, 81–85
        cleaning the ceiling, 129–130
        furniture, 144
        spring cleaning, 127–146

L

Lamp shades, 109
Laundromats, 101, 134
Laundry detergent, 14
Laundry room
        cleaning process, 73–74
        spring cleaning, 120–123
Leather, 20–21
Lighting, 113–114
Lime-A-Way, 17
Limestone, 21
Liquid detergent, 33, 91–92, 111
Living room
        cleaning process, 59–60
        spring cleaning, 105–110
Lysol cleaner, 7, 25, 54, 100

M

Marble, 21
Master bedroom
        cleaning process, 41–43
        spring cleaning, 91–96
Mice, 22
Microfiber cloth, 16, 17, 33, 56, 60, 63, 68, 84

Microwaves, 21–22, 83, 136, 142
Moldings, 22
Mop, 9, 69
Mrs. Meyers, 7–8
Multimedia units, 68
Murphy's Flax Oil Soap, 34

O

Onyx, 23
Oven, 23–24, 83, 136

P

Pantry, 133
Pet stains, 24
Piano, 119–120
Plants, 119
Porcelain, 25
Powdered detergent, 5–6, 20, 60

R

Refrigerator, 25–27, 83, 135, 136, 140
Roaches, 27
Rust, 28

S

S.O.S., 137
Saddle soap, 21
Scheduling, 106, 108
Scrubbing brushes, 8–9
Sealer #2, 21
Shades, 28
Silver, 28
Silverfish, 29
Spot removal, 124
Spring cleaning, 87–146
　　first steps, 87–88

list, 88–89
　the baby's room, 100–105
　the bathroom, 89–91
　the dining room, 110–114
　the entryway, 123–127
　the family room, 114–120
　the kitchen, 127–146
　the laundry room, 120–123
　the living room, 105–110
　the master bedroom, 91–96
　the teenager's bedroom, 96–100
Squeegee, 8, 33, 122
Stainless steel, 29–30, 138–139
Stone Soap Ultra, 21, 23
Stone Technologies, Corp., 21
Stove top, 137–138

T

Tar, 30
Teenager's bedroom
　　cleaning process, 45–47
　　spring cleaning, 96–100
Tilex Mold and Mildew Remover, 6, 56
Tin, 31
Toaster, 135
Tri-sodium phosphate, 13
Twinkle, 15, 29

V

Vacuum cleaner, 9, 84–85
Vinegar, 32

W

Wallpaper, 31–32
Walls, 32
Washer, 33
Wenol, 13
Window cleaner, 6–7
Window treatments, 115–118
Windows, 33, 65, 125, 134–135
Wine coolers, 142
Wood, 34
Woolite carpet cleaner, 14
Wrought iron, 35